THE FIVE

WRITTEN BY

ANTONIO BELSITO IC

00001 - ISBN 978-1-899093-29-8

Printed in the United States of America

ROSMINI TODAY

ANTONIO ROSMINI

The Five Wounds of Holy Church

A PRESENTATION

AA Belsito I.C.

ROSMINI PUBLICATIONS 2016

CONTENTS

THE FIVE WOUNDS OF HOLY CHURCH

Acknowledgement

The author would like to thank J. Anthony Dewhirst, Sr Paulette of Jesus, and Mark Jacques for their help and support.

Foreword

What a loss for the English-speaking world it would be if it did not possess the great works of St. Augustine or of St. Anselm! Scholars and the general public may agree or disagree with their views, but they would certainly be unanimous in proclaiming the beauty, the usefulness, the depth, and the relevance of their writings.

Some thirty years ago, it was decided that the works of Blessed Antonio Rosmini on philosophy, theology, and spirituality should be made available to the English-speaking world for their exceptional originality and their relevance in the modern discussion of all major issues related to the essence and destiny of the human person. It was an extraordinary work of translation from the original Italian of the 19th Century, which demanded great skill, patience, and a most profound love for the mind and heart of Rosmini. It was carried out by two priests of the Institute of Charity, Denis Cleary and Terence Watson, and their patient labors produced exceptional results.

Today, a large number of the volumes have been translated and are available to the English-speaking public from Rosmini Publications. The details of titles and addresses are at the back of this booklet.

Rosmini's books, however, are not easy to read, not only because the subject matter is often very abstract and analyzed from all angles at great depth, but also because Rosmini' style of writing is not readily translatable into modern English.

This is the background to the present series of books on Rosmini's philosophy, theology, and spirituality. They are faithful to the essential features of his thought, yet, they are meant to be easy to read with constant reference to our own times. They serve as introductory works, sufficient to show the power and originality of the thinker and of his approach and solutions to issues which are the object of heated debates today.

The first book in the series is based on the most controversial of his works, *The Five Wounds of Holy Church,* written with great passion and love for the Church but which ended up almost immediately, in 1848, on the Index of Forbidden Books. It was taken off the Index just before Vatican II, and it was known and used as a guide by many of the Fathers of the Ecumenical Council. The spirit of prophecy, however, which animated the book from the moment of its creation, is still evident and very relevant for the Church of today, as Pope Francis's teaching on collegiality, poverty, and the role of the laity amply demonstrates.
AA Belsito

Blessed Antonio Rosmini

Introduction

1. This is undoubtedly the most famous of Rosmini's books, in which he notes defects and abuses in the Church, but in a twofold spirit of suffering and hope. Saddened by the inevitable shortcomings of churchmen, he believed and trusted with complete certainty in the infinite power of the Holy Spirit at work in the Church. It caused him immense personal damage, but he felt that the renewal of the Church was of such great urgency that he had to be prepared to suffer for it. Rosmini borrowed the image of the "crucified Church" from Pope Innocent IV (1243-1254).

2. Rosmini wrote it in 1832, but he did not publish it, *"the time did not seem ripe"*. In 1846, a new Pope was elected, Pius IX *"who seems destined to renew our age and give the Church the impetus for a new, glorious stage of unimaginable development"*. Rosmini published it in 1848 for a circle of friends *"who have shared my sorrow, and now look forward with me in hope"*. It was issued immediately in other editions, against Rosmini's wishes, by pirate publishing houses. It had a swift and wide diffusion. There was also an English edition of the book published in London, translated by an Anglican canon. A curious episode is connected with the Rovereto Edition of 1863, at the time when many Bishops and Cardinals had gathered in Trent for the celebrations of the third centenary of the famous Council of Trent. Some people from Rovereto (Rosmini's birth-place) placed copies of the *Five Wounds* in the rooms of bishops and

Cardinals, but the local priests immediately withdrew the books and made a great bonfire in the courtyard of the Seminary. The people of Rovereto, however, persisted and sentcopies of the book to all bishops and Cardinals world- wide at their own addresses.

3. With hind-sight we can say that the publication of the book in 1848 was a mistake given the agitated political situation in most of Europe. It was bound to raise fierce opposition from all quarters, but especially from the Austrian Government. Austria had invaded and occupied most of North Italy, and viewed Rosmini as a *"most formidable enemy"* and *"the evil genie of Pius IX"* (from a letter of the Austrian Ambassador in Rome, 1849). Rosmini was a subject of the Austrian Empire (Rovereto was under Austria at that time), but he did not hide his strong desire for the independence of Italy as a confederation of free Italian states. Moreover, in the *Five Wounds*, Rosmini called for full freedom of the Church in all rightful things, but especially in the appointment of bishops, and in the full ownership of all Church's properties. Austria, on the contrary, exercised at the time an absolute control over the appointment of bishops in the Austrian Empire, and the clergy and the properties of the Church were dependent on its authority. Rosmini was persecuted all his life by the Austrian authorities.

4. Why were 1848-1849 the worst years for the publication and diffusion of the *Five Wounds of the Church*?

5. Rosmini had been sent to Rome as a special envoy of the king of Piedmont, Carlo Alberto,

with the task of persuading the Pope to grant a Constitution to his Papal States and to accept to be the head of a Confederation of free Italian States. The Pope, who held Rosmini in the greatest esteem, welcomed him and told him to prepare to be made a Cardinal;
everybody at the Curia was sure that Rosmini would be made the next Secretary of State. Unfortunately,the political situation in Rome deteriorated, with the assassination of the Prime minister of the Papal States and a popular uprising. Priests and some Cardinals were killed, and the Pope was forced to flee Rome in disguise. He made his way to the kingdom of Naples and remained at Gaeta for over a year under the protection of the king and of the Austrian Government. He asked Rosmini to follow him to Gaeta, and initially he relied heavily on Rosmini for advice. But things changed drastically for Rosmini with the arrival of
the Austrian ambassador, *"welcomed like a Messiah"*. The Pope was easily persuaded that the safety and security of the Pope and of the Papal States were with the traditional protectors, Austria and Naples and any other Power that opposed movements of independence or of liberalisation. The Pope told Rosmini that he
was no longer a *"constitutionalist"*, and that he had abandoned all his liberal views on politics. Moreover, Rosmini found it almost impossible to approach the Pope, and the Cardinals, led by Cardinal Antonelli, a staunch supporter of Austria, made sure that Rosmini had no influence on the Pope. And indeed, they used the *Five Wounds* as a powerful tool against Rosmini.

6. Rosmini was asked by the Pope, under pressure from some of the Cardinals, to clarify his teaching on the following suspected opinions found in the *Five Wounds*:
   1) The divine right of clergy and people in the election of bishops; 2) The use of the vernacular in the Liturgy;
   3) Criticism of Scholasticism; 4) The separation of Church and State. Rosmini clarified all points and sent a written paper to the Pope. He sent a second letter, but to no avail: people at the papal court made sure that
   no letter from Rosmini ever reached the Pope. Soon afterwards, the police of the kingdom of Naples began harassing Rosmini with the clear intent to have him out of the kingdom and in no position of influencing the Pope.

7. Rosmini left Naples on 15th July 1849. As he was making his way towards Stresa, on 13th August 1849 he received the letter from the Congregation of the Index which stated that, at the order of the Pope, the Congregation had met [in May-June, when Rosmini was still in Naples; the meetings had been kept secret from him] and had decreed that the book *"The Five Wounds of the Church"* had been condemned and placed on the Index of Forbidden Books. The Pope had approved the decree and asked for submission.
   Rosmini submitted at once, *"I had been kept in the dark about the meetings of the Congregation and I was*
   never told the reasons for the condemnation. I sent my full submission... Sit nomen Domini benedictum". He wrote in his letter of submission: *"As a devoted and obedient son of the Holy See, which through the grace of*

God I have always been in my heart and publicly professed to be, I declare that
I submit to the prohibition of this book, absolutely, simply, and as completely as possible, begging you to inform the Holy Father and the Sacred Congregation". A few days later he wrote to the Master of the Sacred Palace: *"I will add that by the grace of God alone, I have never in my life had a temptation against the faith, nor have I ever hesitated a moment to condemn anything that the Holy See might find wrong in my writings or elsewhere"*.

8. No official reason for the condemnation was ever given. Rosmini was assured that no theological errors had been found in the book; his own view was that the book had been condemned because of the pressure of Austria on account of his insistence that the elections of bishops were no matter for the State but for the Church and that clergy and people had a moral divine rightto contribute to the election of their bishops, with the approval and final decision of the Pope.

9. The book was taken off the Index just a few years before Vatican II. It was widely known to the Bishops who took part in Vatican II, and many of the ideas of the book found their way into the final Documents of the Council. Pope Paul VI called *The Five Wounds of the Church "a prophetic book"*. It is the opinion of many that some of the Wounds are still waiting for a cure, and we may need, perhaps, a new Ecumenical Council to tackle them more resolutely. There is hope today that Pope Francis will steer the course of the Church closer to the kind of vision held by the Fathers of Vatican II and by Blessed Rosmini. Many who have read *The*

Five Wounds of the Church and Pope Francis' Apostolic Exhortation *Evangelii Gaudium* have discovered powerful similarities and the same desire for a profound unity of the "faithful" (clergy and people), collegiality, and a Church which is truly evangelical in her poverty and concern for the poor.

10. *The Five Wounds of the Church* is a precious theological book on the Church which Rosmini loved with all his heart. Abandoning the technical and dry language of Neo-Scholasticism, he adopted the passionate and warm language of the Bible and of the Fathers of the Church, the very same language chosen by the Fathers of Vatican II in the writing of the beautiful Documents of the Council. Here are some important points which have been taken up by Vatican II and subsequent Papal Documents:

- The living union of clergy and laity in the one People of God.The active and intelligent participation of all in the Liturgy
- Christianity as a "supernatural" reality and mystery.
- The centrality of Scriptures and of the Sacraments.
- The return to Tradition and to the Fathers of the Church.
- The necessity of a living theology.
- The need for a profound education of the clergy, based on Scripture, Fathers, and Tradition.
- The collegiality of the bishops, with the Pope at the Head of the Collegium.

- The renewed awareness amongst Christians of the Bishop as Father and Shepherd of the local Church, in close union with the Pope and all other Bishops.

- The presence and the consultation of the People of God (clergy and laity) in the election of their Shepherd, the Bishop.

- The responsibility of the whole People of God for the Church.

- The freedom of the Church from political powers and earthly riches.

- The real poverty of Bishop and Clergy, chosen as a vocation.

- The work of charity of the Church for the poor to whom the riches of the Church partly belong. From a historical point of view, Rosmini paid a great price as a result of the condemnation of the book. His reputation as an outstanding Christian philosopher, theologian, and spiritual guide, came under suspicion. Friends deserted him. Some schools of theology stopped teaching his theories. The Institute of Charity, founded by him in 1828, also suffered. Rosminians (as the members are called) were no longer welcomed in some Dioceses, some bishops opposed the opening of new Rosminian houses, and the flow of novices came, for a while at least, to a full stop. The martyrdom of Rosmini and of his Institute came finally to an end in 2001, when the Vatican issued a Declaration, a sort of apology for the treatment of Rosmini. Pope Benedict XVI, on 17 November 2007, fulfilled the wish of John XXIII, Paul VI, John Paul I, and John Paul II and gave Rosmini back to the universal Church by formally declaring him "Blessed".

Beatification of Blessed Rosmini, Novara (Italy), 18 November 2007

The Five Wounds

The wound in the left hand of holy Church:t
The division between people and clergy at public worship

The wound in the right hand of holy Church:
The insufficient education of the clergy

The wound in the side of holy Church:
Disunion amongst the bishops

The wound in the right foot of holy Church:
the nomination of bishops left in the hands of civil government

The wound in the left foot:
Restrictions on free use by the Church of her own possessions

Foundational ideas

Rosmini is not famous for writing books which are easy to read, but this book is the exception. There is much passion and love, and we may call it "an open letter to the Church", an invitation to bring to the fore what is not right within the Church with a view of making it truly the light on the hill top, and the salt of the earth.

The "five" wounds are not isolated from each other. Some scholars think that the most harmful wound, and the source of the other four, is the wound at the heart of the Church, the disunion amongst the Bishops. The word "disunion", however, can be deceptive: it is not simply the fact that Pope, Bishops, Clergy, and the Laity are no longer "one in heart and mind", as it was during the first six centuries of the life of the Church. It is not only the fact that, often, Bishops act as though their exclusive concern is their local dioceses neglecting their responsibility for the Church everywhere, in union with all other Bishops, and with the Bishop of Rome.

The root of disunion is to be found in the weakening of the idea that the Church is a "supernatural" reality based on grace and holiness, a "Sacrament" of salvation for humankind. The Church is not a "human institution", marked by ambition, division, pursuit and accumulation of power and wealth. The Church is "one" body with her Lord, crucified to a bare Cross; it has no other wisdom and power but the wisdom and power of the Cross. Like the ancient Israelites who marched through the desert as "one" body, pitching and striking camp at the command of the Lord, so the Church should be one, Bishops and Laity together, praying and acting in perfect unity.

The golden years of the life of the Church

The first six centuries of the Church were marked by the divine qualities JESUS had left to His Apostles. The Gospel was preached by men imbued with supernatural wisdom and holiness, and their words were like pure light shattering the darkness of confused humanity. Moreover, the vision of truth was given life and power by the Sacraments. Through Baptism, people were lifted to the supernatural world of grace, acquiring new supernatural faculties by which they were enabled to "touch" or to "feel" the triniform God, and to experience the power and the joy of the Spirit. Baptism was the "gate" to the other powerful supernatural Sacraments, especially to the Eucharist.

JESUS' command resounded in all its clarity and strength: *"Go therefore and make disciples of all nations, baptizing them in the name of the Father and of the Son and of the Holy Spirit, and teaching them to obey everything that I have commanded you. And remember, I am with you always, to the end of the age."* (Mt. 28, 19-20)

Preaching and the Sacraments: these were the two essential tools by which the Church was built, shedding light on the mind and real supernatural power on the soul. The heralds of the Gospel took extreme care to safeguard the unity of the Church by appointing shepherds fit for the task, those full of true supernatural wisdom, who combined the pure light of supernatural knowledge with holiness of life.

Early Church Bishops were shepherds according to the heart of JESUS: not only Mark, Luke, Timothy, and Titus, but also Ignatius, Clement, Irenaeus, Papias, Polycarp, Basil, Ambrose, Athanasius, Gregory,

Augustine, etc. were great and holy Bishops, full of divine wisdom, worthy successors of the Apostles of the Lord; they embraced poverty as a mother, and cared for the unity of the whole Church, forming their flock and their priests with a jealous love and commitment.

There was nothing obscure or incomprehensible in the liturgy of the Church: Bishops, Priests, and Laity were one in mind and heart as they celebrated the Sacraments. They spoke the same language, they understood the rites; Bishops used the Bible for nourishing their priests and their flock, as we can see from the marvellous commentaries they left to the Church. The house of the Bishop was the home of his priests, who were formed both by the holiness of his life and his profound and wide understanding of the Scriptures. Priests and Bishops, formed by such great and holy men, formed in turn living Christian communities, rich in faith and love for God and for each other, and nourished by the power of their liturgical celebrations.

The period of decadence

The golden years of the life of the Church came to an end as a result of a wave of invasions of barbarians from the North. The victorious invaders destroyed the mighty Roman Empire, and with it, the universal rule of law and the security guaranteed by the military power of Rome. The fall of the Roman civilization left peoples and nations in ruinous conditions, and they turned to the Church for protection. The barbarian rulers themselves used the Church to calm entire populations, and to receive their cooperation becoming more acceptable in their eyes. All of a sudden, the Church was flooded with riches and honours, and the

Bishops became powerful administrators at the service of the new rulers.

Rosmini sees the hand of God in the overthrow of the pagan Roman Empire. It was a necessary step in order to establish a new world based on Christian principles and values. However, the Church paid a heavy price. The Bishops became lords, immersed in wealth and a style of life which was totally opposed to that of the naked Christ on the Cross. They were no longer Shepherds of their priests and flocks, but distant princes, divided from each other, and corrupted by worldly ambitions.

The corruption of Bishops was followed naturally by the decadence of Priests, and of their communities, deprived of the forming influence of the holy and wise Shepherds of earlier years. The pursuit of holiness, the significance of the beautiful rites of the liturgy, the value of the power of grace and of the supernatural essence of religion, became distant realities left to the individuals rather than to the people of God.

The wounded heart of Christ and of His Church, caused by the pursuit of worldly interests by Bishops, was the source of all other ills: Bishops, no longer holy Shepherds, neglected the formation of their Clergy; poorly educated Clergy, in their turn, became leaders of weak Christian communities marked by their ignorance of holy things and of the life-giving power of the liturgy. Poverty, so dear to Christ and to the early Shepherds, was abandoned by Bishops and Priests who used religion as a means to acquire status and wealth; and with the neglect of poverty, the poor also became a marginalized and despised reality.

The Healing of the Wounds

Pope and Bishops, in perfect union among themselves, full of true supernatural wisdom and holiness, should be the ones to lead the renewal of the Church. Like Peter and Paul, Philip and Matthew, they should be the "new" in the world, born from above and leading nations to the supernatural Kingdom by means of a Spirit-filled preaching and the intrinsic power of the Sacraments; Shepherds who embrace poverty like a mother, and who care deeply for the poor, the abandoned, the marginalized. Pope and Bishops, acting as one body, will attend to the formation of holy and supernaturally wise Priests, to help them in the shepherding of the flock. The formation of the Clergy will be based on the Word of God, and on the appreciation of the inner power of divine grace. Holiness conjoined to true supernatural wisdom should be the mark of the men appointed to lead Christian communities.

The shining example of holy Shepherds, and of Priests and Clergy totally committed to the values of the supernatural Kingdom, will lead the Laity to rediscover the power of their own Baptism, and to participate fully in all liturgical celebrations, thus bringing about that marvelous unity between Clergy and People so much wanted by Christ on "the night He was betrayed".

The Church, poor and naked, like Christ on the Cross, will become the "power" of God in the world, the Sacrament of Salvation, the light of the nations, and the salt of the earth.

The "Sacra di S. Michele", near Turin, entrusted to Rosmini by King Charles Albert of Piedmont in 1835

The First Wound

The Wound in the left hand of holy Church: the division between People and Clergy at public worship

28,000 people (Cardinals, Bishops, Priests, Deacons, and the Laity) participated with joy in the celebration of the Liturgy of the Beatification of Blessed Antonio Rosmini in 2007

"All the faithful, clergy and people, represent and form in the Church the marvelous unity indicated by Christ when He said, "Where two or three are gathered in my name, in agreement about ***everything*** *they ask, there am I in their midst".*

Rosmini had a very lofty view of the dignity of the Laity.

The "faithful", for Rosmini, are the **clergy and the laity together**, representing and forming in the Church the marvelous unity indicated by Christ when He said, *"Where two or three are gathered in my name, in agreement about everything they ask, there I am in their midst"*. Christ demanded unity of minds and hearts, the clergy and the people acting together *"as one man"*, as Scripture says of the ancient Israelites.

This is what Rosmini wrote about the dignity of the Laity: *"There are always holy, prudent men and women with the sense of Christ among them. The people are a part of the mystical Body of Christ; together with their pastors and incorporated with the Head, they form a single Body. In Baptism and Confirmation they have received the impression of an indelible, priestly character... The ordinary Christian possesses a mystical, private priesthood giving him special dignity and power, and a feeling for spiritual things. The clergy has its rights, but so have the Christian people. For example, the Christian people can and must oppose a bishop openly teaching heresy. Their sense of the supernatural teaches them to do this, and gives them the right to do it. The Fathers of the Church taught that the people's part in the choice of their Pastors derived from the divine law..."* Rosmini wrote this in 1832, unique among all Christian writers of the time in stressing the universal participation of all baptised in the mission of Christ, being with Him Priests, Prophets, and Kings.

The early Christians, the Apostles and the believers, were *"one in heart and mind"*, they acted as one Body. Why? They believed the same truths, they took part fully, body and soul, in their liturgies, the Eucharist and the Sacraments. Everyone understood what was being said and done.

JESUS came to save the whole person, body and spirit.

The Gospel had to appeal to both elements of human nature, to the mind and to the heart. The Apostles were indeed sent out to "preach", to instruct people. But they did not found a school of philosophy, nor did they perform miracles simply to prove the truth of what they preached, nor gave examples of great virtues to persuade their listeners. If they had presented Christianity as a doctrine, as truths to be believed, they would not have achieved much. Their appeal would have been greatly reduced.

What did the Apostles do to save the whole person, intellect and feeling, mind and heart, and to submit the whole world to a cross?

JESUS' command was, *"Go out into the whole world and* ***make disciples*** *of all nations,* ***baptising*** *them in the name of the Father, and of the Son, and of the Holy Spirit".* His command was to "speak" to the intellect by the way of preaching, and to regenerate the will, to touch the heart, to speak to feeling by "baptising", by the Sacraments, by the acts of worship of the New Testament. The Sacraments were the mysterious rites and powerful works by means of which the Apostles reformed the whole world. *"The Sacraments were words and signs of God, creating a new soul, creating new life, new heavens and a new earth. The Apostles added to their preaching Catholic worship, which consists principally in the Sacrifice of Mass, the Sacraments, and the prayers in which these are expressed".*

The Apostles added prayers, ceremonies, noble rites, but they introduced nothing devoid of meaning. Worship was not a spectacle, and people were not to be present to look but they were in God's temple to be an important element in worship. The sublime worship of holy Church is thus a single action of clergy and people together.

"The people, wrote Rosmini, *should be actors as well as hearers, while in fact they are mostly present at Mass like the columns and statues of the building".* They should have a profound understanding of the mysteries, prayers, symbols, rites, that make up Catholic worship. *"The separation of the laity from the Church at worship through lack of comprehension is the first of those gaping wounds dripping with blood in the mystical Body of Jesus Christ".*

Rosmini is keen to reassure those who, through no fault of theirs, simply cannot make sense of what goes on in Church, for the Spirit *"helps us in our weakness; for we do not know how to pray as we ought; but the Spirit himself intercedes for us with sighs too deep for words".* The voice of simple, uneducated people, if prompted by the Spirit, penetrates heaven itself. However, worship is a common act of clergy and people, and it is together that we approach the throne of grace, it is with as much understanding on our part as it is possible that fervour, appreciation, reverence, and devotion increase. Love grows between clergy and people and amongst the people.

What were the reasons for such painful and unhappy division in the Church?

1. **The first cause of the wall of division was the lack of full, living instruction amongst Christians.** Christ exhorted "preaching", in the first place: the people should receive the truths of the Gospels, being educated in their faith, in the Scriptures, in the traditions, in morality. He then added to "baptise" them, that is, to worship through the Sacraments

which are simply the powerful realities of what has been taught. The teaching should be completed and made life giving by the participation in Catholic worship.
Rosmini approved of Catechisms so long as they were much more than simple repetition of formulae, or abstract summaries.

Faith is a living reality, and the communication of the truth must be coupled with the experience of supernatural power through worship. There cannot be full participation in the Liturgy without solid knowledge of the truths of the faith. This profound insight, which Rosmini drew from the early Church, had been lost for many centuries. Today, we are far more aware of the intimate link between catechesis and worship, especially when we prepare adults for Baptism.

2. **The second reason for the division was that Latin, used in worship, had ceased to be the language of the people**. The understanding of words is essential to grasp the power of the Sacraments; people and clergy cannot pray with one heart and one mind if the words used in prayers are not understood. The demise of Latin as a living language was caused by the invasion of barbarians as well as other factors, but it was a fact.

Rosmini was asked expressly by the Pope to repudiate the view, attributed to him by his critics that he was in favor of introducing the vernacular into the liturgy. Rosmini presented various reasons why Latin should be kept and the vernacular should not be introduced.

Advantages of keeping the Latin language in

worship: Reason to Keep Latin!

- Latin reflects the immutability of the faith.
- Latin unites many different Christian peoples in a single rite.
- Latin signifies the unity and greatness of the Church and common brotherhood.
- Latin produces an over-worldly, super-human atmosphere.
- Latin gives the joy of knowing that the saints and people of the past prayed with the same words and expressions as we do today.Disadvantages of the vernacular:
- There are too many modern languages, creating division in the Church.
- Modern languages are variable and unstable, resulting in constant changes to the words of the liturgy, thus unsettling the people at worship.
- Modern languages lack the precise terminology for lofty theological concepts.

Rosmini thought that priests should make a greater effort to make people understand the liturgy and the words used. He was not in favour of the use of the vernacular, although, perhaps, he would not have objected to its introduction. He called for a profound education of priests, so that they, who are meant to be the salt and light of the Christian community, are enabled to foster tirelessly the greatest participation of the laity in the Mass and Sacraments. *"Unfortunately"*, Rosmini added, *"the insufficient education of the clergy is the second Wound of the Church"!*

Rosmini was ordained a priest in 1821. In his diary he wrote, *"From this hour I must be a new man, live in heaven with heart and mind, converse always with Christ, despise and flee from the things of earth. I must return from the altar a saint, an apostle, a man of God"*. St. John Bosco, who was helped by Rosmini on many occasions, said of him, *"I have never seen a priest say Mass with more devotion than Fr. Rosmini"*.

Resonance of "The Five Wounds" in the Documents of Vatican II

From the Constitution on Sacred Liturgy

"Day by day the liturgy builds up those within the Church into the Lord's holy Temple". (2)

"Those who received the word were baptized. They continued steadfastly in the teaching of the Apostles and in the communion of the breaking of the bread". (6)

"The sacred liturgy does not exhaust the entire activity of the Church. Before men can come to the liturgy they must be called to faith and to conversion: "How then are they to call upon him in whom they have not yet believed? But how are they to believe him whom they have not heard? And how are they to hear if no one preaches? And how are men to preach unless they be sent?" (Rom. 10:14-15) (9)

"Mother Church earnestly desires that all the faithful should be led to that fully conscious, and active participation in liturgical celebrations which is demanded by the very nature of the liturgy. Such participation by the Christian people as "a chosen race, a royal priesthood, a holy nation, a redeemed people (1 Pet. 2:9; cf. 2:4-5), is their right and duty by reason of their baptism.(14)

"In the restoration and promotion of the sacred liturgy, this full and active participation by all the people is the aim to be considered before all else; for it is the primary and indispensable source from which the faithful are to derive the true Christian spirit; and therefore pastors of souls must zealously strive to achieve it, by means of the necessary instruction, in all their pastoral work.

Yet it would be futile to entertain any hopes of realizing this unless the pastors themselves, in the first place, become thoroughly imbued with the spirit and power of the liturgy, and undertake to give instruction about it. A prime need, therefore, is that attention be directed, first of all, to the liturgical instruction of the clergy." (14)

"Priests, both secular and religious, who are already working in the Lord's vineyard are to be helped by every suitable means to understand ever more fully what it is that they are doing when they perform sacred rites; they are to be aided to live the liturgical life and to share it with the faithful entrusted to their care." (18)

"With zeal and patience, pastors of souls must promote the liturgical instruction of the faithful, and also their active participation in the liturgy both internally and externally, taking into account their age and condition, their way of life, and standard of religious culture. By so doing, pastors will be fulfilling one of the chief duties of a faithful dispenser of the mysteries of God; and in this matter they must lead their flock not only in word but also by example." (19)

"In this restoration, both texts and rites should be drawn up so that they express more clearly the holy things which they signify; the Christian people, as far as possible, should be enabled to understand them with ease and to take part in them fully, actively, and as befits a community." (21)

"To promote active participation, the people should be encouraged to take part by means of acclamations, responses, psalmody, antiphons, and songs, as well as by actions, gestures, and bodily attitudes. And at the proper times all should observe a reverent silence." (30)

"Particular law remaining in force, the use of the Latin language is to be preserved in the Latin rites. But since the use of the mother tongue, whether in the Mass, the administration of the sacraments, or other parts of the liturgy, frequently may be of great advantage to the people, the limits of its employment may be extended." (36)

Second Wound

The wound in the right hand of holy Church: the insufficient education of the clergy

Ordination of priests in Nairobi

"Only great men can form great men"

1. Preaching and the Liturgy were the two great schools open to the Christian people in the finest period
of the history of the Church. The *whole* person was addressed, by the Word of God that spoke to the *mind* and by the efficacy of the rituals, symbols, actions of the Sacraments, of the Eucharist in particular, which touched the *heart*. The preachers

of the Word were holy men pouring upon their listeners their own overflowing spiritual abundance. We have a description of the Eucharist as celebrated by the early Church which contains the two fundamental elements, words and actions: *"On the day which is called after the sun, all who are in the towns and in the country gather together for a communal celebration. And then the memoirs of the Apostles or the writings of the Prophets are read, as long as time permits. After the reader has finished his task, the one presiding gives an address, urgently admonishing his hearers to practice these beautiful teachings in their lives. Then all stand up together and recite prayers. When the prayers are concluded we exchange the kiss. Then someone brings bread and a cup of wine mixed with water. He who presides takes them and offers praise and glory to the Father through the name of the Son and of the Holy Spirit and for a considerable time he gives thanks (in Greek 'eucharistian') that we have been judged worthy of these gifts. When he has concluded the prayers and thanksgivings, all present give voice to an acclamation by saying, Amen. When he who presides has given thanks and the people have responded those whom we call deacons give to those present the "eucharisted" bread, wine and water and take them to those who are absent. Besides, those who are well-to-do give whatever they will. What is gathered is deposited with the one presiding, who therewith helps orphans and widows..."* (St. Justin, 150AD).

2. Priests came from these fervent Christian communities, who participated fully in the liturgy and who had absorbed the power of the Gospel in their lives. This fact helps explain why some outstanding members of such communities, by

common request, were elevated from humble laymen to bishops, within a few days: see for example, St. Ambrose, St. Alexander, St. Martin, and St. Peter Chrysologus.

3. The clergy are no better than the faithful, says Rosmini. It is the community that generates priests, a great Christian community will generate great priests, and a feeble Christian community will generate feeble priests.

4. Rosmini lamented that the Christian communities of his time had been neglected by the clergy to such a point that liturgies were no longer understood, that knowledge of the Word was minimal, and that the people of God had been reduced to spectators at the celebration of the Sacraments, unable to participate because of widespread ignorance. What kind of clergy would emerge from such weak communities? **"The first grade of priesthood is the Christian himself"**: a weak Christian will become a candidate to the priesthood, not understanding the liturgy nor the Word of God, attracted by the privileged or superior status of the priest in society not by the love of God
   and of the people; such a candidate will become a weak priest, who in turn will lead weaker congregations and instruct new weaker candidates.

   "How can we begin to instruct and form in a truly outstanding, priestly tradition such ill-prepared candidates? They are ignorant of basic elements that should be presumed present in them, they have no idea of the kind of knowledge required of priests, no idea of what they are about to undertake as candidates for the

priesthood. The poverty and misery of ideas which form the preparation and training of modern ecclesiastics produces priests ignorant of the nature of Christian laity, of Christian priesthood and of the sacred bond between them. Ministers with petty hearts and narrow minds, they grow up as priests and leaders of churches, educating priests weaker and baser than themselves".

5. This pitiful situation, for Rosmini, goes back to the Dark Ages of European history, which began towards the end of the sixth century after Christ. The sustained invasions of barbarians from the North and the East brought about, progressively, radical changes in many aspects of the life of the Church, including the formation to the priesthood. He considered the first six centuries as being the golden age of the life of the Church. His historical analysis includes the following points.

6. Priests in the early Church were taught by the best men the Church possessed. The "seminary" was the house of the Bishop. Priests and deacons lived with their bishop in a community of faith and love. They learned from their bishop the love for the Scriptures, the burning zeal for the Church, the care for the poor. Augustine was the educator of a great number of priests and bishops, who lived with him in his house. Similarly Athanasius, Alexander, Sixtus, Jerome, Irenaeus, Pantaenus, Hermas: they educated great priests and bishops, having themselves been educated by other great bishops. **"Only great men can form great men"**, says Rosmini. The Apostles had started the process: Timothy, Titus, Mark, Evodius, Clement, Ignatius,

Polycarp, all of them bishops of the early Church, had been educated by the Apostles themselves. Irenaeus was in turn educated by Polycarp:

"I remember even the place where blessed Polycarp sat when he preached the Word of God. I remember vividly the gravity with which he moved from place to place, his sanctity in everything he did, the dignity of his features and bearing, the many exhortations he preached to his people. I can almost hear the way in which he described his conversations with St. John and others who had seen JESUS".

These holy bishops reserved the education of priests to themselves, and educated them through the holiness of their life and the profound knowledge of the Scriptures. Their holy way of life guaranteed both the unity of priests with their bishops, and the teaching of the same doctrines.

8. **This golden era came to an end with the invasions of barbarians that brought chaos and destruction everywhere**. Societies crumbled, and the people gathered for reassurance around their bishops and priests, who became the mediators between the people and their new barbarian rulers. The Church was thus suddenly flooded with worldly honors and riches flowing in of their own accord. The bishops became functionaries of the new states, with great power and wealth, no longer free but subject to their rulers. They became detached from their priests, who also became further divided between higher and lower clergy, competing against each other in

the acquisition of riches. Bishops ceased to be loved and followed as Shepherds, they became feared as rulers, distant, surrounded by armies and courtiers. The common life of bishop and priests ceased, and pastoral care was left to the lower clergy, attracted now to the priesthood not by holy men and a holy way of life but by greed and ambition.

9. Rosmini sees the Providence of God guiding events, even when such events caused profound wounds to the Church. As a result of the involvement of bishops and priests in the ruling structures of a society dominated by the cruelty and ignorance of the barbarian rulers, the Christian principles of love of neighbour, of social justice, of the rights of persons, of meekness and concern for the poor and the sick, were slowly embraced transforming society from within.

10. Not all bishops and priests welcomed the opportunity for power and influence that the political change had brought with it. Rosmini mentions the lament of St. Gregory the Great, who ruled the Church during this period, inconsolable at the sight of the dangers of the new world:

    "Dressed as a bishop I have returned to the world. Modern conditions subject me in my pastoral duty to more cares than I ever had in my life as a layman... The waves of business which fall upon me from all sides, and the flood of fortune which submerges me, provide ample reason for saying, I have come into deep waters, and the flood sweeps over me. Earthly business makes it impossible for me not only to preach about the Lord's

miracles, but even to meditate upon them".

The irony of the situation was that whereas bishops often relished their new status, power, and wealth, the converted rulers consecrated their crowns to the Church and their highest glory was to be children and tributaries of the Church. During this period, almost every throne in Europe had a saint as sovereign.

11. Abandoned by their bishops, now more princes and rulers of this world than spiritual leaders, and lacking proper formation, priests reached such level of degradation that they fell in the estimation of the people and dedicated themselves to making money in every way, using the holy things at their disposal. Sales of relics, of sacraments, of indulgences became widespread, and vice and ignorance became common.

12. The Council of Trent tried to remedy this appalling situation by devising the foundation of seminaries where candidates to the priesthood could be given appropriate training. Unfortunately, teachers lacked the greatness of the bishops of the early Church:

"Compare the teachers – says Rosmini – if you want to have some idea of the disciples! On one side you have the bishopsof long ago, or some of the most famous men in the Church; on the other, the young professors in our seminaries. What a contrast!"

Teachers of seminaries, says Rosmini, had no experience of life, of parish, of pastoral work. They had erudition but no wisdom; they knew by heart formulae and summaries of doctrine, but they had no real understanding of the great mysteries of the faith.

13. Moreover, the texts used in seminaries were useful for erudition but not for educating priests in a way of life centred on Christ and on his teaching. The texts used were *"petty, one-sided works, without warmth or attraction, the offspring of narrow minds"*, which generated in students a hatred for learning, for life!

14. Scripture was the sublime textbook for the early Church, which inspired knowledge and faith at the same time. The Fathers of the Church used Scriptures for all their teaching, all of them nourished themselves and their disciples with the living waters of the Word of God. The greatest commentaries on the Bible originated among these holy men, and indeed all the great works of theology had holy bishops as their authors.

15. The works of **the Fathers** became in turn textbooks for candidates to the priesthood for the next five centuries, but after teaching them with very few new contributions, even the study of the Fathers became stale and repetitive.

16. The next stage was the introduction of Compendia of doctrines, the Summae, which initiated the period of **Scholasticism**. The first Summa was that compiled in the 12th century by the Master of Sentences, Peter Lombard. It was an excellent idea to epitomize the teaching scattered amongst the extensive writings of Church tradition, but at the expense of leaving out that which touched the heart. Scholasticism spoke to the mind, detaching itself from real life, from feelings, from the soul.

"Knowledge grew but wisdom decreased", said Rosmini. The Schools acquired the narrow, restricted character that helped form the students into a class separate from other human beings. The Summae reached the heights of their perfection in the 13th century with the marvelous work of St. Thomas
Aquinas, immensely profound and solid, that spoke to the heart as well as to the intellect.

17. If Scholasticism had diminished Christian wisdom by stripping it of everything related to feeling and moral efficacy, its disciples continued to curtail it, removing from it all that was profound, intimate and substantial.
Its great principles were avoided, apparently to make things easier but in fact because they were not
understood. The successors of the Scholastics, the new **theologians**, as Rosmini calls them, reduced Christian doctrine to feeble formulae, and isolated conclusions. They produced textbooks incapable of educating candidates:

"These books will be judged the most miserable, feeble works written in the eighteen centuries of the Church's history.
They lack spirit, principles, style and method".

It was not surprising therefore, that learning theology and living a Christian life had become so disjointed. There was no substance, no nourishment for the soul in such books, and the students could afford to learn definitions without having to question the poor level of morality in their lives. The "education" of priests in ancient times was very different: the method, in those days, was to unite

knowledge to virtue, to acquire true wisdom, to study and lead holy lives at the same time, one aspect feeding from the other. The imitation of Christ was
being sought, His divine Words and His mighty deeds learned and lived, and love for God, for the Church, for the poor pursued with the same enthusiasm as love for the Scripture and for all true knowledge.

18. In summary, Rosmini gives four reasons for the insufficient education of the clergy:
    - Candidates to the priesthood come from weak Christian communities;
    - Weak, feeble candidates are taught by weak, feeble priests;
    - The poverty of textbooks used in training priests;
    - Lack of adequate method, disjunction between learning and moral life.

For Rosmini, the Episcopate is responsible for bringing about the "healing" of this wound; but the Bishops must take action together and agree on principles and methods; they must be the light on the mountain top leading their priests by the example of their common holiness and unity. Unfortunately, this essential unity among bishops is what is lacking; thus, the disunion among the bishops is the most serious wound in the crucified body of the Church.

Resonance of "The Five Wounds" in the Documents of Vatican II

From the Decree on Priestly Formation of Vatican II (Optatam Totius)

"Animated by the spirit of Christ, this sacred synod is fully aware that the desired renewal of the whole Church depends to a great extent on the ministry of its priests. It proclaims the extreme importance of priestly formation" (Introduction)

"A special "program of priestly formation" is to be undertaken by each country or rite. It must be set up by the episcopal conferences, revised from time to time and approved by the Apostolic See." (1)

"The task of fostering vocations devolves on the whole Christian community, which should do so in the first place by living in a full Christian way... Families which are alive with the spirit of faith, love, and reverence serve as a kind of introductory seminary... Parishes rich in vitality foster vocations among their young people" (2)

"All priests especially are to manifest an apostolic zeal in fostering vocations and are to attract the interest of youths to the priesthood by their own life lived in a humble and industrious manner and in a happy spirit as well as by mutual priestly charity and fraternal sharing of labor." (2)

"Major seminaries are necessary for priestly formation. Here the entire training of the students should be oriented to the formation of true shepherds of souls after the model of our Lord Jesus Christ, teacher, priest and shepherd. They are therefore to be prepared for the ministry of the word: that they might understand ever more perfectly the revealed word of God; that, meditating on it they might possess it more firmly, and that they might express it in words and in example." (4)

"Since the training of students depends both on wise laws and, most of all, on qualified educators, the Superiors and professors of seminaries are to be selected from the best men, and are to be carefully prepared in sound doctrine, suitable pastoral experience and special spiritual and pedagogical training." (5)

"The Bishop with his constant and affectionate interest should show himself a true father in Christ to the students" (5)

"Spiritual formation should be closely linked with doctrinal and pastoral training... They should be taught to look for Christ, to live in constant companionship with the Father, through Jesus Christ His Son, in the Holy Spirit" (8)

"Conformed to Christ the Priest through their sacred ordination they should be accustomed to adhere to Him as friends, in an intimate companionship. They should so live His paschal mystery themselves that they can initiate into it the flock committed to them. They should be taught to seek Christ in the faithful meditation on God's word, in the active participation in the sacred mysteries of the Church, especially in the Eucharist" (8)

"The students should understand most clearly that they are not destined for domination or for honors but are given over totally to the service of God and to the pastoral ministry. With a particular concern they should be so formed in priestly obedience, in a simple way of life and in the spirit of self-denial that they are accustomed to giving up willingly even those things which are permitted but are not expedient, and to conform themselves to Christ crucified." (9) "The students are to be formed with particular care in the study of the Bible, which ought to be, as it were, the soul of all theology. After a suitable introduction they are to be initiated carefully into the method of exegesis; and they are to grasp the great themes of divine revelation and to receive from their daily reading of and meditating on the sacred books inspiration and nourishment." (16)

"That pastoral concern which ought to permeate thoroughly the entire training of the students also demands that they be diligently instructed in those matters which are particularly linked to the sacred ministry, especially in catechesis and preaching, in liturgical worship and the administration of the sacraments, in works of charity, in assisting the erring and the unbelieving, and in the other pastoral functions. They are to be carefully instructed in the art of directing souls." (19)

From the Decree on the ministry and life of priests (Presbyterorum Ordinis)

"Blessed Paul, the doctor of the Gentiles, "set apart for the Gospel of God" (Rom 1:1) declares that he became all things to all men that he might save all.(17) Priests of the New Testament, by their vocation and ordination, are in a certain sense set apart in the bosom of the People of God. However, they are not to be separated from the People of God or from any person; but they are to be totally dedicated to the work for which the Lord has chosen them." (3)

"Their ministry itself, by a special title, forbids that they be conformed to this world; yet at the same time it requires that they live in this world among men. They are to live as good shepherds that know their sheep." (3)

"God, who alone is holy and who alone bestows holiness, willed to take as his companions and helpers men who would humbly dedicate themselves to the work of sanctification. Hence, through the ministry of the bishop, God consecrates priests, that being made sharers by special title in the priesthood of Christ, they might act as his ministers in performing sacred functions." (5)

"Although they have obligations toward all men, priests have a special obligation to the poor and weak entrusted to them, for our Lord himself showed that he was united to them and their evangelization is mentioned as a sign of messianic activity." (6)

"All priests, in union with bishops, so share in one and the same priesthood and ministry of Christ that the very unity of their consecration and mission requires their hierarchical communion with the order of bishops." (7)

"Priests are made in the likeness of Christ the Priest by the Sacrament of Orders, so that they may, in collaboration with their bishops, work for the building up and care of the Church which is the whole Body of Christ, acting as ministers of him who is the Head." (12)

"Since they are ministers of God's word, each day they

read and hear the word of God, which it is their task to teach others. If at the same time they are ready to receive the word themselves they will grow daily into more perfect followers of the Lord." (13)

"Priests, moreover, are invited to embrace voluntary poverty by which they are more manifestly conformed to Christ and become eager in the sacred ministry. For Christ, though he was rich, became poor on account of us, that by his need we might become rich." (17)

Third Wound

The wound in the side of holy Church: disunion among the bishops

Pope and Bishops expressing "collegiality"at the Second Vatican Council

The six golden links

The word "collegiality" has often been heard since Vatican II. What does it mean? It is the doctrine finally hammered out at Vatican II according to which the bishops form a college which, together with its head, the Pope, governs the Church. *"The Order of bishops is the successor to the college of the Apostles in their role as teachers and pastors, and in it the apostolic college is perpetuated. Together with their head, the Supreme Pontiff, and never apart from him, they have supreme and full authority over the universal Church"* (Lumen Gentium, 22).

Tensions between the primacy of the pope and the collegiality of bishops have always been very strong. Significantly, Vatican II needed to stress that the bishops are all truly "vicars and legates of Christ" and not "vicars of the Pope". The document on the Pastoral Office of Bishops in the Church (Christus Dominus) explains the collegiality of all Bishops in these terms:

"The bishops themselves, however, having been appointed by the Holy Spirit, are successors of the Apostles as pastors of souls. Together with the supreme pontiff and under his authority they are sent to continue throughout the ages the work of Christ, the eternal pastor. Christ gave the Apostles and their successors the command and the power to teach all nations, to hallow men in the truth, and to feed them. Bishops, therefore, have been made true and authentic teachers of the faith, pontiffs, and pastors through the Holy Spirit, who has been given to them.

Bishops, sharing in the solicitude for all the churches, exercise this episcopal office of theirs, which they have received through episcopal consecration, in communion with and under the authority of the supreme pontiff. As far as their teaching authority and pastoral government are concerned, all are united in a college or body with respect to the universal Church of God." (2)

However, as recently as 1996, retired Archbishop John Quinn complained that the papal curia too often considered itself superior to the college of bishops and so hindered the development of collegiality. As yet, there are few collegial structures, apart from an

Ecumenical Council. The Synod of bishops established by Pope Paul VI is an advisory body: "It is not a collegial organ of leadership for the universal Church" (J Ratzinger). The perfect union of bishops among themselves and with the pope in a Collegium is still some way off. Many believe that Pope Francis will take more decisive steps towards giving "collegiality" the necessary importance and structure. There is no doubt that immense progress has been made on healing this "wound" since the time of Rosmini: bishops meet more regularly at every level, many of them know each other quite well; through national Conferences of bishops common documents are approved and promoted. Yet do bishops feel that each of them is responsible not only for his own diocese but for the universal Church? Are there structures that allow them to govern together the universal Church, under the leadership of the Pope?

Rosmini claimed that "collegiality" or the union of all bishops was practised by the bishops and popes of the first six centuries of the Church. It was only when the bishops entered into the political arena that the evil of disunion and conflict plagued the Church right up to his own time. **This is his historical analysis:**

1. JESUS, before His passion and death, begged the Father to form his apostles into a perfect unity. Unity in the divine nature of the blessed Trinity is the source of unity within the Episcopate of the Church.

2 The Apostles guarded jealously their unity and the unity of their churches. Their interior unity was guaranteed by their communion of doctrine and sacraments; their exterior unity by the powerful links among the Apostles and their leader, Peter

and later by their successors.

3. Although scattered throughout many nations, bishops were conscious of forming a single body of the highest authority. Their hearts and minds were dominated
by this great concept of unity, and they used every possible means to bind themselves together. All maintained exactly the same faith, and love for each other.

4. How was this perfect unity achieved? Rosmini mentions **"six golden links"** that bound bishops together in perfect unity.
   - **The bishops knew one another personally.** Titus, Timothy, Polycarp, Ignatius, Irenaeus, John Chrysostom, Gregory of Nyssa, Gregory of Nazianzus, St. Valerian were bishops who knew
personally many other holy bishops even before they became bishops. It was well known that the house of St. Augustine was the house where many future holy bishops were formed. These great bishops formed other great bishops and kept their profound ties of Christian love and friendship.
   - **The bishops, even the most isolated, were in constant correspondence,** although they lacked the means of communication available to us. The letters of bishops were read reverently at public assemblies. The Apostles wrote letters to their churches, other bishops following their examples: Clement, Ignatius, Soter, Athanasius, John Chrysostom, etc. The letters written by Ignatius to various churches as he was taken to Rome for his martyrdom (to the Ephesians, Magnesians, Trallians, Romans, Philadelphians,

and Smyrneans) are particularly moving. In his letter to the church in Rome St. Denis says, *"Today we have celebrated the Lord's Day, and have read your letter. We shall continue to read it for the sake of our instruction, as we do with the letters already sent to us by Clement"*. Seven letters of this great bishop of Corinth are extant, written to different churches: to the Romans, the Lacaedemonians, the Athenians, the Nicodemians, the Pontians, the Creteans, the Gnossians. **The bishops visited one another out of mutual charity, or from zeal for church affairs.** Their devotion embraced the universal church even more than the particular church entrusted to them. They were conscious of being bishops of the Catholic Church, and they realised that one diocese cannot be separated from the entire body of the faithful just as a limb cannot be cut off from the human body. Each local Church embodied the totality of the reality which is the Church, but their bishops were aware of the fundamental necessity of being one with the other bishops and with the bishop of Rome. The holy Bishop and Martyr Cyprian, who wrote a book on the "Unity of the Church", wrote in one of his letters, *"Although we are many Shepherds, yet the flock we feed is one, and we must gather and look after all the sheep which have been redeemed by the precious Blood of Christ"*.

- **Assemblies and Councils, especially provincial councils, were held frequently**. Bishops of a province sought each other for advice, for clarifying doctrine, for finding common solutions. Bishops would consult regularly with their priests and with the people, giving them an account of their government. The people's assent on all matters was valued so highly that if they rejected a bishop they were not forced to accept him and another suitable person was appointed in his place. St. Cyprian wrote to his priests, *"At the beginning of my episcopacy I decided not to make any decision without your advice and the assent of the people"*. St. Augustine followed the same rule, and provided detailed accounts of what he was doing or wanted to do. *"For you I am the Bishop, with you I am a Christian"*, he told his priests and his people.

- **The metropolitan bishop had authority over the bishops of a province,** while greater sees had several provinces and metropolitans subject to them. This arrangement provided for uniformity in doctrine and in practice and strengthened the bonds among churches and bishops.
- **The overall authority of the Pope was the foundation rock of the unity of the universal Church.** In all their serious needs bishops and churches of the entire world appealed to him as to a father, judge, teacher, leader, centre and common source. Rome was seen as the great see where sound doctrine and the unity of the Church on earth could be found visibly in the successor of St. Peter. The pope was the symbol of unity of the universal Church, and bishops made continuous pilgrimages to Rome to pray over the tomb of St. Peter and to report to the Pope.

This golden era of the Church came to end after six centuries. The same destructive force that was responsible for the insufficient education of the clergy was also the cause of the progressive disunion among the bishops, namely, the end of the Roman Empire and the sustained invasions of barbarian kings, with the establishment of the feudal system.

In the crumbling of the old systems, the bishops became the intermediaries between the people and the barbarian rulers and they were forced to enter the political arena acquiring in the process power, wealth, and privileges. The "Christianisation" of Europe was the result of the presence and influence of bishops and clergy in public administration, but such involvement brought also evil consequences for the Church.

The bishops soon learned to love their new political status, and surrounded themselves with courtiers, armies, and all the externals that they envied in royal princes. They devised protocols, invented titles, built palaces, and generally, distanced themselves both from their lower clergy and from the people. Avarice, hatred, disharmony, lust, licentiousness became widespread among them, as they had been made subservient to their rulers who guaranteed their position. **"They became slaves of men dressed in soft garments rather than free apostles of a naked Christ".** The bishops' political involvement and power was the cause of profound disunion among them. Rosmini mentions the efforts of some of the ambitious bishops of Constantinople and Ravenna, and of anti-popes, to secure more power for themselves and for their particular political rulers; and the birth of "nationalistic" churches ruled by bishops who were more loyal to their kings than to the pope and to the Gospel.

The bishops' accumulation of wealth and power was

envied not only by the people and the clergy but became soon attractive to the nobility and to the kings, many of whom at different stages in history robbed the bishops of all their properties. The response of the bishops was to defend their riches by means of "excommunications", thus making one thing of their private wealth and of the Church, causing great damage to the unity and prestige of the Church.

Rosmini claims that the catholic faith might have been saved in nations like Denmark, England, and Germany if the Church had been freed of the wealth that endangered it. *"But is it really possible to find an immensely wealthy clergy courageous enough to impoverish itself, or even with enough sense to understand that impoverishing the Church is to save her?"*

The Church longs for freedom not for wealth. Free from all political interference, and free from political involvement and wealth, the Bishops, poor and simple like the Apostles, would once again become a beacon of communion among themselves and ready to pursue with vigor the preaching of the Kingdom of God to all creatures. However, to achieve this political disentanglement, the election of bishops must be the exclusive concern of the Church, and this cannot be achieved unless a fourth wound is first brought to full healing.

Resonance of "The Five Wounds" in the Documents of Vatican II

From the Dogmatic Constitution on the Church (Lumen Gentium)

"Therefore, the Sacred Council teaches that bishops by divine institution have succeeded to the place of the apostles, as shepherds of the Church." (20)

"Just as in the Gospel, the Lord so disposing, St. Peter and the other apostles constitute one apostolic college, so in a similar way the Roman Pontiff, the successor of Peter, and the bishops, the successors of the apostles, are joined together." (22)

"The order of bishops, which succeeds to the college of apostles and gives this apostolic body continued existence, is also the subject of supreme and full power over the universal Church, provided we understand this body together with its head the Roman Pontiff and never without this head." (22) "The collegial nature and meaning of the episcopal order found expression in the very ancient practice by which bishops appointed the world over were linked with one another and with the bishop of Rome by the bonds of unity, charity, and peace" (22)

"Indeed, the very ancient practice whereby bishops duly established in all parts of the world were in communion with one another and with the Bishop of Rome in a bond of unity, charity and peace, and also the councils assembled together, in which more profound issues were settled in common, the opinion of the many having been prudently considered, both of these factors are already an indication of the collegiate character and aspect of the Episcopal order; and the ecumenical councils held in the course of centuries are also manifest proof of that same character." (22)

"The Roman Pontiff is the perpetual and visible source and foundation of the unity of the bishops and of the faithful... Each individual bishop represents his own Church, but all of them together in union with the pope represent the entire Church" (23)

"Bishops are united in a college or body... The Episcopal order is the subject of supreme and full power over the universal Church. But this power can be exercised only with the consent of the roman pontiff" (22)

"Bishops should always realize that they are linked one to the other, and should show concern for all the churches". (23)

"From this it follows that the individual bishops, insofar as their own discharge of their duty permits, are obliged to enter into a community of work among themselves and with the successor of Peter, upon whom was imposed in a special way the great duty of spreading the Christian name." (23) "The pastoral office or the habitual and daily care of their sheep is entrusted to them completely; nor are they to be regarded as vicars of the Roman Pontiffs, for they exercise an authority that is proper to them, and are quite correctly called "prelates," heads of the people whom they govern" (27)

From the decree on the Pastoral Office of Bishops in the Church (Christus Dominus)

"Bishops, sharing in the solicitude for all the churches, exercise this episcopal office of theirs, which they have received through episcopal consecration,(6) in communion with and under the authority of the supreme pontiff. As far as their teaching authority and pastoral government are concerned, all are united in a college or body with respect to the universal Church of God." (3)

"Together with its head, the Roman pontiff, and never without this head it exists as the subject of supreme, plenary power over the universal Church." (4)

"As legitimate successors of the Apostles and members of the episcopal college, bishops should realize that they are bound together and should manifest a concern for all the churches." (6)

"As those who lead others to perfection, bishops should be diligent in fostering holiness among their clerics, religious, and laity according to the special vocation of each.(11) They should also be mindful of their obligation to give an example of holiness in charity, humility, and simplicity of life." (15)

"Bishops should always embrace priests with a special love since the latter to the best of their ability assume the bishops' anxieties and carry them on day by day so zealously. They should regard the priests as sons and friends(13) and be ready to listen to them. Through their trusting familiarity with their priests they should strive to promote the whole pastoral work of the entire diocese." (16)

"From the very first centuries of the Church bishops, as rulers of individual churches, were deeply moved by the communion of fraternal charity and zeal for the universal mission entrusted to the Apostles. And so they pooled their abilities and their wills for the common good and for the welfare of the individual churches. Thus came into being synods, provincial councils and plenary councils in which bishops established for various churches the way to be followed in teaching the truths of faith and ordering ecclesiastical discipline.

This sacred ecumenical synod earnestly desires that the venerable institution of synods and councils flourish with fresh vigour." (36)

Pope Francis on Collegiality

On July 28th, 2013, Pope Francis affirmed in the Press Conference during the Return Flight form the Apostolic Journey to Rio on the Occasion of the

XXVIII World Youth Day:

«The steps I have taken during these four and a half months come from two sources: the content of what had to be done, all of it, comes from the General Congregations of the Cardinals. There were certain things that we Cardinals asked of the one who was to be the new Pope. We asked, for example, for the Commission of eight Cardinals, we know that it is important to have an outside body of consulters, not the consultation bodies that already exist, but one on the outside. This is entirely in keeping with the maturing of the relationship between synodality and primacy. In other words, having these eight Cardinals will favour synodality, they will help the various episcopates of the world to express themselves in the very government of the Church. The second source has to do with present circumstances. The first is the problem of the IOR, that is to say, how to manage it, how to conceptualize it, how to reformulate it, how to put right what needs to be put right».

Fourth Wound

The wound in the right foot of holy Church: the nomination of bishops left in the hands of civil government

The struggle for supremacy during the Middle Ages

No man can serve two masters

For over a thousand years, and at the time of Rosmini, emperors, kings, and political rulers had arrogated to themselves by force or had been given by the Church under duress the right to nominate bishops for the dioceses in their countries. The Pope was given the right or reserved to himself the right to "confirm" their nominations. This is the "wound" Rosmini is highlighting in this chapter, but in presenting it and in giving a most painful historical account of the way a "free" Church became enslaved to civil governments, he also suggests that the Church ought to go back to the practice of the early Church when bishops were elected by the clergy and the people. It was this second issue that fired up people's and theologians' thinking right up to our own times, and that became one of the focal points that brought about the condemnation of the book.

For Rosmini, the clergy and the people had a "divine" right to elect their shepherd. He was asked by the Pope, Pius IX, to clarify this theological point which seemed to declare "invalid" the election of bishops nominated by rulers only, with the final approval of the Pope. Other bishops and theologians made the same request, and Rosmini obliged by publishing three letters written to Canon Giuseppe Gatti. He distinguished between **"divine constitutive right"** and **"divine moral right"**. The right clergy and people have in the elections of bishops is "divine moral right" and the violation of this right does not cause "invalidity"; the Pope has indeed the authority to by-pass this right of clergy and people if pressed by other serious considerations. Therefore the elections of bishops nominated by civil powers were indeed "valid" if they have been confirmed by the Pope, in line with what had been stated by the Council of Trent. The violation of a "divine constitutive right" does render "invalid" the action of whatever is being violated, but this is not the case of the divine moral right of clergy and people to elect their bishop.

Rosmini, therefore, claims only a "divine moral right" for the election of bishops by clergy and people. But it is a very serious right, of "divine" origin, and therefore it ought to be exercised unless other very urgent considerations intervene. Rosmini justifies the Popes who permitted the interference of civil governments in the election of bishops on the ground that they believed permission to be "the lesser evil": "*As far as the choice of bishops was concerned, the Church never spontaneously offered the nomination of all episcopal sees of certain states to the lay power unless constrained, by bitter circumstances and after long struggles, to make such a sacrifice*".

What about today? Most civil governments have, thankfully, surrendered the "privilege" of electing their own bishops, recognising the freedom of the Church in such important matter; we say "most" because we are aware that State interference has not ceased everywhere, for instance in China, Cuba, and States with a totalitarian regime. But, what can we say about the "divine moral right" of clergy and people to elect their bishops?

We need to be clear that Rosmini did not mean that people have a direct part in the government of the Church. He proposed a return to the ancient custom of election by clergy and people. This only gave the people the opportunity of expressing their opinion of the candidates, of testifying to their good character, and of welcoming the person enjoying their confidence.

Rosmini went as far as to suggest a method that could be followed in the election of the bishop by clergy and people. Registers should be opened in each parish of the diocese "*where the faithful who so desired could give their opinion about the choice of bishop, indicate the canonical irregularities incurred by those who might be chosen, and nominate the priest they think most worthy to be future pastor of the diocese*". Prayers should be said in the diocese for the best outcome. The registers are closed after eight days by the parish priests who would convene "twelve of the older parishioners" and the other priests in the parish to scrutinize the results, to discuss and send them forward. The clergy meets at the Cathedral, the various parish priests are heard, the names of those chosen by the people are made public to the assembled canons and priests. The assembly cast their votes on the priests of their own choice, and if the names deriving from both elections (people, priests) are the same then the assembly progresses to the next stage, otherwise they study the results and try to work out which is the name that has the most votes. If the clergy does not approve any of the top names elected by the people they must give reasons and put forward their own names. The people's chosen names and the clergy's, or the name of the one who has been chosen by the majority of both groups are then sent to the Metropolitan bishop who will meet with other provincial bishops "as arbiters". The bishops themselves may propose other more worthy priests, if necessary, and they will submit the names proposed by the three groups of electors to the Pope, as the supreme judge. The Pope in any case will make the final decision.

It is obvious that what really counts is the principle rather than the method, and the principle is the absolute right of the Church to appoint its Bishops, in full freedom and without interference. In stressing this point, Rosmini provides a harrowing account of the long and dramatic struggle between Church and State over the right of the election of bishops and abbots.

The first six centuries were the golden period of the Church: the Church was poor but free, and the original structures set up by the Apostles and their immediate successors were followed everywhere: the bishop was elected by clergy and people. Rosmini provides plenty of evidence for his assertion, starting with the Church of Rome in the West, the Church of Alexandria in the East, and the influential Churches of Africa.

1. St. Clement, pope and martyr, and immediate disciple and successor of St. Peter, wrote in his letter to the church of Corinth: *"Our apostles knew through our Lord Jesus Christ that there would be disagreement about the nomination of future bishops. Because of this, they handed down a rule for future succession: bishops must be outstanding men elected with the consent and approbation of the whole church"*. The Apostolic Constitution, attributed to St. Peter, states, *"I, Peter, as first among you, declare that the person to be ordained bishop is to be without fault in all things, and chosen by all the people as the most worthy... The president of the assembled Christians must ask the priests and the people if this is their choice. If they agree, he goes on to ask if all witness to the person's worthiness for such an office... When they have agreed for the third time, let the person be elected."* St. Clement and his successors remained faithful to this tradition as we can see from the acts of St. Cornelius, Julius, Zosimus, Boniface, Celestine, Leo the Great, Hilarius, Hormisdas, Gregory the Great, Hadrian I, Gregory VII, Urban II, Pascal II and innumerable others. All these witnesses strongly defended the tradition of the election of bishops by clergy and people.

2. What was the Alexandrian tradition about the active presence of the Christian people in the

election of bishops? St. Athanasius and Origen spoke diffusely of the same tradition in the election of bishops. Origen wrote: *"When a bishop is ordained the people must be present so that all may know and be sure that the most worthy, learned, holy and virtuous person amongst them has been chosen for the priesthood in the presence of all. Thus, there will be no reproaches later, nor doubts about the bishop. The Apostles insisted on this when speaking about the ordination of bishops".* Also St. Athanasius, *"When the people have gathered the ordination should be carried out in the presence of the people and of the clergy. The emperor Constance – Athanasius laments – thought he would change the law of God by violating the Lord's statutes handed down through the Apostles. He sent bishops backed by the military to unwilling people great distances away. His only recommendation and notification were threats and letters to the magistrates".* Athanasius regarded such false bishops as "intruders" and "wolves".

3. The churches of Africa testify to the same unbroken tradition. St. Cyprian wrote, *"We recognize that choosing a bishop in the presence and sight of all the people, when his worthiness and suitability are supported by public witness and testimony, comes down to us from divine authority... What we hold to in all our provinces as the rightful celebration of ordination is to be preserved and held as of divine and apostolic observance. The people for whom the new leader is ordained, the bishops of the provinces are to gather so that the bishop may be chosen in the presence of the people who are fully conversant with the life of individuals and aware of how each has behaved himself".*

History shows as an undeniable fact that in the greatest

Churches founded by the Apostles, in the churches of Rome, Alexandria, Antioch, Constantinople, Ephesus, Caesarea, Heraclea, Corinth, Thessalonica, Carthage and others, the people took an active part for many centuries in the ordinary choice of bishops. A bishop without the support and approval of the people was considered an unlawful usurper.

This tradition remained secure and universal during the first six centuries of the Church. The invasions of barbarian armies which brought to an end the old Roman Empire caused dramatic changes in the Church especially in her status as a poor but free Mother of all her subjects. The new barbarian rulers favored the Church with wealth and power while at the same time enslaving her through the bishops who became progressively political princes subjected to the authority of the rulers. **The battle with secular powers over the choice of bishops lasted many centuries.** The Church defended herself with decrees and canons, and strong statements from many Councils. Pope Symmachus, for example, in 500AD published a Decree in the presence of 218 bishops which declared: *"We cannot permit any power of decision in the Church to those whose duty it is to follow rather than to command"*, and then goes on to confirm the ancient manner of choosing bishops with the consent of the clergy and people. Gregory the Great wrote in 593, *"Inform clergy and people of the city immediately to agree about a choice of bishop, and send the decree of election so that he may be ordained with our consent, according to ancient practice. Above all, be careful not to allow royal power or patronage from highly placed persons, to have any influence in the election"*.

Yet all the efforts to safeguard this fundamental

principle of freedom for the Church produced few results before determined and powerful kings and princes bent on accumulating all authority and dominion on themselves. They spoke initially of "royal assent" to the ordination of bishops, and later they considered bishops as their subjects and their properties as properties of the king. It happened on many occasions that at the death of a bishop the king would not appoint a new bishop for a long period so that he might enrich himself with the revenues of the dead bishop's properties. It happened that the king would offer the office of bishop to the highest bidder; and because ordinary priests also shared church revenues, kings decided that the Church should no longer have the right to ordain even a humble priest without the king's permission.

Freedom of choice in Episcopal elections was almost totally lost by the beginning of the 11th century. Abbot Ingulf, a contemporary of William the Conqueror, thus described conditions in England: *"For years now, there has been no free, canonical election of prelates; Episcopal and abbatial office has been conferred at the pleasure of the royal court by investiture with the ring and the pastoral staff"*. It is worth reading the sad pages produced by Rosmini as evidence of what he says, particularly the heroic acts of Hincmar, the holy archbishop of Reims, and of Pascal II.

It was Gregory VII who brought to an end this long, sad period of the history of the Church. We will not go into the details of Gregory's battles against kings and princes of his time, especially with emperor Henry IV, who allegedly stood barefoot for three days in the snowy ground outside Gregory's palace at Canossa before he admitted him and received from him unreserved manifestations and words of sorrow for the damage he had inflicted to the Church by his arrogance in selling Episcopal sees and prompting bishops to defy the Pope. In one of Henry IV' s letters to the Pope, before his act of submission at Canossa, we read, *"Our Lord the king commands you to resign from the apostolic see and the papacy, which is his, and cease cluttering up this holy place"*! Rosmini claims that the real struggle between "priesthood" and "empire" was in reality a struggle between corrupt bishops refusing reform and the Church wishing to reform them. Behind every ambitious king in Europe there were many corrupt bishops far more loyal to the crown than to the Church, who constantly advised their kings on how to grab more power from the Church.

After Gregory's victory over the empire, there followed a relatively calm time for the Church, during which ancient traditions and disciplines were re-established. However, after a century or so, *"the devil found a new and more subtle means for disturbing the peace and prosperity of the Church: unlimited reservations"*. The Church had triumphed with Gregory VII, and she gained in prestige and power. She used the power to concentrate into the hands of the Pope all the right of appointment of bishops and abbots everywhere. This accumulation of power on the papacy generated immense resentment among Christians, and they reacted "with disgust rather than anger" at the sight of the supreme leaders of the Church reserving all privileges to themselves in order to acquire more wealth and authority.

The bishops gathered at the Council of Basel attacked papal reservations, causing kings and rulers everywhere to demand from the Pope acknowledgement of their rights and privileges. A terrible consequence of this was the surrender, once again, to secular powers of the nominations of bishops. Resultant treaties forced the relinquishment by the popes of a large part of the freedom of choice of Episcopal appointments. The nomination of bishops was granted to the king; the Holy See simply retained its power to confirm the nomination. *"In effect, the new style of discipline, which still prevails and causes one of the most painful and bitter wounds in the crucified Spouse of Christ, divided the "reservations" between sovereigns and popes".*

This was the situation at the time of Rosmini. He makes a powerful case inviting kings and emperors to give up their ill-gotten privilege to nominate bishops. He reasons with them and argues that it is in their best interest to let the Church of God be free to choose her bishops. He lists four fundamental principles in the election of bishops which, he argues, can be fulfilled by the Church, not by the State:

1. **"The best person available should be chosen as bishop"**: who is in the better position to judge the qualities required of a bishop, the Shepherd of his flock, who leads his people on the way to holiness by sound doctrine and moral up righteousness? The answer is evident.

2. **"The priest chosen should be known, loved and wanted by those whom he has to govern"**: the church's desire to have as father and pastor the priest with whom it feels most at home is good and reasonable; but if rulers nominate the bishops, the people's wishes are rarely listened to.

3. **"The priest chosen as bishop should have been**

enrolled for a lengthy period amongst the clergy of the diocese he is to govern, and not be sent there as a stranger from a distant country": it is in the best interest of the local church that the person who is going to be the father of all is known to all. Rulers follow favoritism and personal interest, not the interest of the people.

4. **"Generally speaking, only the moral body or moral person concerned is capable of judging what is best for itself"**: the Church is a spiritual and moral reality, and her interest and mission differ widely from the preoccupations of civil governments. The Church knows what is best for her, and the Christian people know what is in their best interest in matters related to their salvation.

Finally, Rosmini, after giving his full approval to the maxim established by Leo the Great, **"The person governing all should be chosen by all"**, sums up the duties and rights of the people of God in the election of their bishop:

- **To bear witness to the virtue and suitability of the bishop they are to receive**. They have the right to make known defects as Cyprian says, "so that in the people's presence good and evil may be discerned".

- **To express their desire and request for the bishop whose virtues they witness to.** The bishops of Alexandria in supporting the election of St. Athanasius maintained that he became bishop *when "the entire crowd, together with the whole assembly of the catholic church, united as one body and soul, cried out and shouted for Athanasius as bishop of the church.*

They publicly begged this of Christ, and beseeched us for it for many days and nights, neither leaving the church nor allowing us to leave it. We ourselves, this city, and the whole of the province are witnesses of the fact".

- **To refuse a bishop who has been chosen, provided the refusal is the work of the majority or the more reliable part of those belonging to the diocese.** St. Celestine prescribed that *"no bishop shall be given to people unwilling to receive him"*. This is a kind of veto recognized by the Church as a right belonging to Christian people.

Resonance of "The Five Wounds" in the Documents of Vatican II

From the Decree on the Pastoral Office of Bishops in the Church (Christus Dominus)

"In exercising their office of father and pastor, bishops should stand in the midst of their people as those who serve. Let them be good shepherds who know their sheep and whose sheep know them. Let them be true fathers who excel in the spirit of love and solicitude for all and to whose divinely conferred authority all gratefully submit themselves" (16) "Bishops should always embrace priests with a special love since the latter to the best of their ability assume the bishops' anxieties and carry them on day by day so zealously. They should regard the priests as sons and friends(13) and be ready to listen to them." (16)

"In discharging their apostolic office, which concerns the salvation of souls, bishops per se enjoy full and perfect freedom and independence from any civil authority. Hence, the exercise of their ecclesiastical office may not be hindered, directly or indirectly, nor may they be forbidden to communicate freely with the Apostolic See, or ecclesiastical authorities, or their subjects." (19)

"Since the apostolic office of bishops was instituted by Christ the Lord and serves a spiritual and supernatural purpose, this most sacred ecumenical Synod declares that the right of nominating and appointing bishops belongs properly, peculiarly, and of itself exclusively to the competent ecclesiastical authority. Therefore, for the purpose of duly protecting the freedom of the Church and of promoting more suitably and efficiently the welfare of the faithful, this most holy Council desires that in future no rights or privileges of election, nomination, presentation, or designation for the office of bishop be any longer granted to civil authorities. Such civil authorities, whose favourable attitude toward the Church this most sacred Synod gratefully acknowledges, are most kindly requested to make a voluntary renunciation of the above-mentioned rights and privileges which they presently enjoy by reason of a treaty or custom". (20)

Fifth Wound

The wound in the left foot: restrictions on the free use by the Church of her own temporalities

The Cell of Blessed Antonio Rosmini at Calvario

The Early Church was poor but free

The modern reader of the Five Wounds will find this chapter very challenging for the Church. The first "four wounds" are indeed all relevant today, and there is still a long way to go before the "healing" process has been accomplished. But there is greater awareness of the importance of finding efficient remedies, and Vatican II has certainly produced outstanding documents that reflect the serious intent of the Church to reform herself from within.

Even from a cursory reading of the pages of the fifth wound it is clear that Rosmini's vision of the Church is that of the Spouse of Christ embracing the same poverty of her Bridegroom, who said, *"Foxes have holes, and birds of the air have nests; but the Son of man has nowhere to lay His head"*. Rosmini asks that popes, bishops, and priests embrace evangelical poverty, as was the case in the early Church. *"The profession of poverty was for long the glory of the priestly ministry; the majority of men called to the priesthood abandoned their possessions or gave them away to the poor... The outstretched hands of the poor, of widows, lepers, slaves, pilgrims and the destitute became vaults where the Church could deposit her treasures without fear of theft"*.

Few people today would readily agree that the official Church is poor. Popes, bishops, priests, religious orders, are not seen as the best examples of poverty, with a few exceptions. The general consensus is that the clergy is at least comfortably off, very often better off, and occasionally rich. This perception may well be inaccurate but is often repeated; and many find unconvincing the defense that being poor today simply means living by the same standards of the majority of the people that are being served. Some argue that Christ and the Apostles chose to live not according to prevailing standards; they chose the poverty of the poor, and their precarious existence.

The early Church was poor, but free. **Her evangelical poverty was safeguarded by seven maxims which regulated the acquisition, administration and use of material goods.** Rosmini explains these ancient maxims with a passionate plea that the Church of his time, the Church of our time, should embrace them once again if she is to be the salt of the earth and the light of the world.

1. **The first requirement was that all offerings to the Church had to be "spontaneous"**. Christ obliged the faithful to maintain those working for the gospel, but He appealed to the faithful's free acceptance of His gospel, and to their moral response. St. Paul, although acknowledging that he had the moral right "to food and drink" for preaching the gospel, seldom used it preferring to work hard for his food and the food of his own companions. Moreover, the obligation that Christ imposed on the faithful of maintaining the clergy did **not extend beyond the strict needs of the preachers**
of the gospel, *"Remain in the same house, eating and drinking what they may provide"*. This maxim is stressed by Tertullian at the beginning of the third century, *"Each one who can, puts aside some money monthly, or when he decides. No one is forced; all give spontaneously.*
These funds are the investments of piety". **Spontaneity only ceased when the offerings were enforced by sanctions imposed by the secular arm.** This came about with the advent of "feudalism" in the 8th century. For Rosmini, "feudalism" was an unmitigated disaster for the Church, the most profound cause of all of the five wounds of the Church.

"Feudalism – says Rosmini – extinguished the freedom of the Church and gave rise to all her afflictions". Barbarian kings considered themselves the owners of everything within their territories, including all church properties. They distributed favours to bishops and expected in return total subjection and loyalty to them. Barbarian rulers considered both people and properties "theirs" by right

of conquest. *"We can easily imagine what occurred when Church properties were no longer free possessions of the Church, but held under the dominion of temporal rule. Offerings were extracted by force, the only power of coercion available and understood by the secular arm"*. The use of force changed the whole nature of the offerings to the clergy.

The faithful resented being forced to give, and their attachment and love for their clergy disappeared. The clergy were now guaranteed a constant income which did not depend on the amount of work they were doing. Moreover, all donations to the Church were seen as ultimately the property of the feudal ruler who could take over such donations at will. This "evil seed", says Rosmini, brought about the confiscations of the goods of monasteries and churches all through the succeeding centuries, including the then recent decree of 2nd November 1789 in which the national assembly in France declared all Church properties to be at the disposition of the State.

2. **The second maxim protecting the Church from corruption was that goods should be possessed, administered and dispensed in common.** Initially the faithful brought the proceeds of what was sold and laid it at the apostles' feet. Distribution was made to each as any had need. We can only admire the love and union between the believers, and wonder at the common life amongst clergy and faithful. This requirement was preserved for a long time. The bishops, as successor of the Apostles, normally distributed each month what was necessary for the maintenance of the clergy who

worked for the gospel in their dioceses. The funds came from church possessions; no one had anything of his own. When Constantine permitted wills to be made in favour of the Church in 321, he laid down, *"Everybody is entitled to leave the property he wishes to the holy and catholic council of the Catholic Church"*.

The emperor Valentinian made a law forbidding legacies in favor of individual members of the clergy; St. Ambrose and St. Jerome approved of the law. Goods held in common and administered by the wise love
of bishops after consultation with their clergy were of great assistance in producing and safeguarding increased union amongst the clergy, and between the clergy and the people. All of this came to an end with feudalism, which involved vassalage, servitude to the ruler, who became the master of all that the bishops owned. The bishop, with his possessions, became an isolated individual, a man like everyone else, a courtier sharing the luxury of court life, perhaps the leader of soldiers. As the bishop became lord or baron on his own behalf and that of his ruler, the Church ceased to be visible in him; he was no longer bishop and leader of his church, and of the people once united with him. *"This tremendous, unnatural transformation of churchmen impressed the mind of medieval bishops with the idea of their own individuality, and weakened the notion of unity in the Episcopal and clerical body. It broke up dioceses according
to state and feudal boundaries; eventually, almost all church property came to be administered and enjoyed by individual clerics"*.

3. **The third, precious maxim was that the clergy should use church goods only for the strict needs of their maintenance; the remainder was to be applied to pious works, especially in alms for the poor.** Christ founded the apostolate on poverty, and on abandonment to Providence, He himself was the perfect example. Hence in the finest period of the Church, entering the ranks of the clergy was equivalent to a profession of evangelical poverty. The profession of poverty was for long the glory of the priestly ministry; the majority of men called to the priesthood abandoned their possessions or gave them away to the poor.

   These men never used the wealth of the Church for their own benefit as though it belonged to them, but accepted it in trust for the poor. The bishop, as first amongst the poor and the one responsible for distribution, could rightly take something for himself and the clergy. Rosmini quotes Julian Pomerius, a disciple of St. Augustine, who after praising St. Paulinus and St Hilary who had embraced poverty from a very wealthy background, wrote: *"It is easy to understand how holy men like these (who had renounced everything to become followers of Christ) were perfectly aware that the Church's possessions belong to the poor. They never used this wealth for their own benefit, but accepted it in trust for the poor"*. Feudalism brought to an end this blessed period. When bishops and priests became subject to their political masters, the goods entrusted to the Church by the generosity of the faithful "instead of flowing down to the poor, either remained stationary or finished in the rapacious hands of the local lord", and the poor ceased to be a sacred charge consigned to the care of the churches.

4. **The fourth requirement governing Church goods and safeguarding the integrity of the clergy was that ecclesiastical wealth used for pious, charitable purposes, should also be assigned to fixed, determined works to prevent arbitrariness and self- interest from interfering with the management of the goods.** In the early Church resources were allotted to definite purposes according to a fourfold division: for the support of the bishop, the clergy, the poor, and the upkeep of church buildings and cult. *"It is certain – says Rosmini – that the best remedy against the corruption accompanying riches was the establishment of laws at various Councils regulating the precise uses to which they could be applied"*. The corruption and ruin of many ancient monasteries is to be attributed to the lack of precise purposes to direct the great riches possessed by religious houses. As a result, abbots and other superiors controlling finances spent the income as they pleased. Feudalism destroyed the fourfold fair distribution of the Church possessions, accumulating instead all wealth into the hands of the few and powerful.

The fifth requirement safeguarding the Church from the danger of riches was "a generous spirit, prompt to give, slow to receive". The great rule fixed in human hearts was Christ's noble words, "It is more blessed to give than to receive". Bishops considered money and

administration a burden, to be borne only for motives of charity. St. Ambrose refused legacies and donations if he knew that poor relatives of the donor would suffer as a result. St. Augustine had to defend himself against the accusation, "Bishop Augustine gives with total generosity, but takes nothing". What a glorious accusation, says Rosmini! Augustine said that he would gladly have lived on collections from God's people rather than be burdened with responsibility
for finances, which he was ready to cede to the people so that all God's servants and ministers might live by sharing at the altar. But the laypeople refused his offer absolutely. It is truly painful, and damaging to the true interests of the Church, as well as scandalous, if
public opinion is generally convinced that the Church's hands are always extended to receive, but never to give. It is sad to find people thinking that what the Church puts in her treasure never leaves it; the result is contempt, envy, the elimination of generosity amongst the faithful, and the suspicion that the Church's wealth goes on accumulating over the centuries irrespective of the needs of the poor.

5. **The sixth requirement compelled the Church to make public the administration of all her possessions.** In the early Church bishops consulted the clergy and the people on all matters, including the use of the wealth of the Church. Moreover, the priests and deacons in charge of the administration had to be approved by
the whole church, according to Apostolic tradition. St John Chrysostom was not afraid to give an account of his administration of church income:

"We are ready to inform you of our administration". The same spirit and practice animated all early bishops.

The people who make the offering should also be aware of what is being carried out. Rosmini suggests that the people should be involved from the beginning, from selecting the special works to which funds are
to be allocated to receiving a full account of the way money have been handled. Religious orders, who distinguish themselves by the making of a vow of poverty, should be the first to give a thorough account of how funds are invested and used. By making all finances public, the Church would shine before the world, and the temptation of using funds unworthily would be considerably weakened. *"An obligation to present the faithful, and the general public, with an account of their administration would provide the stimulus necessary for awakening many drowsy consciences, and ensure that church offices were in the hands of honest, sincere, devout persons"*.

6. **The seventh and last requirement is that the Church should administer her goods watchfully and carefully.** What the Church owns belongs to God and to the poor, and she has to give a strict account to God of how she has administered God's possessions. It
is true, says Rosmini, that through the centuries the voracious rapacity of rulers and States has robbed the Church of so much of her possessions. However, perhaps, much squandering of her wealth has been caused by churchmen who have used it for their own selfish purposes and as though it belonged to them.

Rosmini adds, *"If we consider what the Church has received during the centuries of her existence, and how much has been lost through lack of serious, careful administration, we can only imagine where the Church would be now if her possessions had always been wisely administered"*. In modern times, the social teaching of the Church has certainly awoken consciences everywhere. From the Rerum Novarum, to the Mater et Magistra, to the Pacem in Terris, to the Populorum Progressio the Church has spoken most eloquently in favour of the poor, the oppressed, the economically disadvantaged of the world. Throughout the centuries, the Church has been the strongest defender and a mother to the sick, the marginalised, and the rejected. Of all human institutions, is there any that can be compared to the Church in her dedication and commitment to the poor throughout her long history?

And yet, Rosmini's plea that the Church herself needs to make an examination of conscience and assess herself against the seven maxims that helped her in ancient times to live according to the evangelical poverty willed for her by the divine Founder, sounds very true and relevant, today as in his own time. The documents of Vatican II speak about evangelical poverty when they deal with the religious life. For Rosmini, however, evangelical poverty is a characteristic, a quality, a requirement of the whole Church. It is the Church that has to be poor, and the seven maxims should become working guidelines for the whole Church.

Resonance of "The Five Wounds" in the Documents of Vatican II

From the Dogmatic Constitution on the Church (Lumen Gentium)

"Just as Christ carried out the work of redemption in poverty and persecution, so the Church is called to follow the same route that it might communicate the fruits of salvation to men. Christ Jesus, "though He was by nature God... emptied Himself, taking the nature of a slave", and "being rich, became poor" for our sakes. Thus, the Church, although it needs human resources to carry out its mission, is not set up to seek earthly glory, but to proclaim, even by its own example, humility and self-sacrifice. Christ was sent by the Father "to bring good news to the poor, to heal the contrite of heart", "to seek and to save what was lost". Similarly, the Church encompasses with love all who are afflicted with human suffering and in the poor and afflicted sees the image of its poor and suffering Founder." (8)

"The bishops, in a universal fellowship of charity, should gladly extend their fraternal aid to other churches, especially to neighboring and more needy dioceses in accordance with the venerable example of antiquity." (23)

"In virtue of their common sacred ordination and mission, all priests are bound together in intimate brotherhood, which naturally and freely manifests itself in mutual aid, spiritual as well as material, pastoral as well as personal, in their meetings and in communion of life, of labor and charity." (27)

From the Decree on the Life and Ministry of Priests (Presbyterorum Ordinis)

"For priests who have the Lord as their "portion and heritage," (Num 18:20) temporal goods should be used only toward ends which are licit according to the doctrine of Christ and the direction of the Church.

Ecclesiastical goods, properly so called, according to their nature and ecclesiastical law, should be administered by priests with the help of capable laymen as far as possible and should always be employed for those purposes in the pursuit of which it is licit for the Church to possess temporal goods-namely, for the carrying out of divine worship, for the procuring of honest sustenance for the clergy, and for the exercise of the works of the holy apostolate or works of charity, especially in behalf of the needy. Those goods which priests and bishops receive for the exercise of their ecclesiastical office should be used for adequate support and the fulfilment of their office and status, excepting those governed by particular laws. That which is in excess they should be willing to set aside for the good of the Church or for works of charity. Thus they are not to seek ecclesiastical office or the benefits of it for the increase of their own family wealth. Therefore, in no way placing their heart in treasures, they should avoid all greediness and carefully abstain from every appearance of business." (17)

"Priests, moreover, are invited to embrace voluntary poverty by which they are more manifestly conformed to Christ and become eager in the sacred ministry. For Christ, though he was rich, became poor on account of us, that by his need we might become rich. And by their example the apostles witnessed that a free gift of God is to be freely given, with the knowledge of how to sustain both abundance and need. A certain common use of goods, similar to the common possession of goods in the history of the primitive Church, furnishes an excellent means of pastoral charity. By living this form of life, priests can laudably reduce to practice that spirit of poverty commended by Christ." (17) "Led by the Spirit of the Lord, who anointed the Saviour and sent him to evangelize the poor, priests, therefore, and also bishops, should avoid everything which in any way could turn the poor away. Before the other followers of Christ, let priests set aside every appearance of vanity in their possessions. Let them arrange their homes so that they might not appear unapproachable to anyone, lest anyone, even the most humble, fear to visit them." (17)

DELLE

CINQUE PIAGHE

DELLA

SANTA CHIESA

Trattato

DEDICATO AL CLERO CATTOLICO

LUGANO

The first edition of the Five Wounds of Holy Church, published in Lugano, Switzerland, 1848

Brief Biography of Blessed Antonio Rosmini

1797 - 24th March: Antonio Francesco Davide Ambrogio Rosmini was born at Rovereto, a small town in Trentino, North Italy. The Rosmini family enjoyed great wealth and belonged to the nobility of the Austrian Empire. His father, Pier Modesto, was an upright and conservative man, and his mother, Giovanna dei Conti Formenti, was an amiable woman, discreet, warm, educated, and very religious. Antonio had an older sister, Gioseffa-Margherita, and two younger brothers, Giuseppe and Felice (the latter died during the first year of his life).

25th March: Antonio was baptised on the feast of the Annunciation of the Blessed Virgin Mary.

1804-1812 His father chose a public school for Antonio rather than private education at home by tutors, as was the custom for aristocratic families. He had a happy childhood, with a special gift for friendship.

1812-1814 Antonio studied the Humanities and Rhetoric in the Gymnasium at Rovereto. During 1813-1814 he wrote "A Day of Solitude", and in 1813 he wrote in his Personal Diary, "This year was for me a year of grace: God opened my eyes over many things, and I knew that there is no true wisdom but in God". This was the start of his priestly vocation.

1814-1816 His parents decided not to send him to Trento. He studied Philosophy, Mathematics, and Physics at Rovereto with a smallgroup of friends, and the course was done privately, in the house of his cousin Antonio Fedrigotti, guided by the priest Pietro Orsi.

1816 12th August: Antonio took his examinations in Literature, History, Philosophy, Mathematics, Geometry, Algebra, and Physics at the Imperial Lyceum at Trento achieving brilliant results.

22nd November: Rosmini arrived at Padua to study Theology at the University. He met Niccolo' Tommaseo, who became a life-long friend.

1818 16th and 17th May: Antonio received the tonsure and the Minor Orders. He
planned with friends to write a Christian Encyclopaedia in answer to the atheist "Encyclopedie" written by Diderot and D'Alembert.

1819 21st November: he returned to Rovereto to prepare for the priesthood. He made plans for a "Society of Friends".

1820 January: his father, Pier Modesto, died at the age of 75, leaving Antonio heir of the Rosmini Serbati fortune.

24th February: He accompanied his sister Gioseffa Margherita to Verona to visit the holy Countess Maddalena of Canossa. She invited Rosmini to found a religious Institute for men, in line with her own religious Institute for women. He declined, for the time being.
September: Gioseffa Margherita opened a new orphanage for girls in Rovereto, andAntonio wrote for the occasion the book, On Christian Education, a gift to his sister,

1821 21th April: Antonio was ordained priest at Chioggia, and on 3rd of May he celebrated a solemn Mass in his parish Church of St.
Mark in Rovereto. In line with his "principle of passivity", he withdrew quietly, engaging in the task of purification, acquisition of virtues, and union with God, and waiting for God to call him into action.

1822 During Lent, the Bishop sent him to Lizzana, as a helper to the dying parish priest.

22nd June: He discussed his doctoral thesis, "De Sibyllis lucubratiuncula" [on pagan prophecies foretelling the coming of Christ] and was declared Doctor of Theology and Canon Law.

1823 6th - 29th April: the Patriarch of Venice, Mons. Ladislaus Pyrcher, asked Antonio to accompany him on his journey to Rome.
Pope Pius VII encouraged Rosmini to write books.

20th August: at the death of Pius VII, the priests in Rovereto asked Rosmini to preach the Panegyric on the holy and glorious memory of Pius VII. In it, he elevated to God a passionate prayer for the independence of Italy, which marked the start of the persecution of Rosmini by the Austrian authorities.

1824 His sister, Gioseffa Margherita, joined in Verona the religious Institute founded by the Countess Maddalena of Canossa. Gioseffa

Margherita died in 1833 at the age of 39, consumed by her dedication and love for the poor.

1825 He wrote the book, On the Unity of Education, and another on Divine Providence, which would become the second volume of his Theodicy.

10th December: he wrote in his Diary, "On this day I conceived in a flash the plan of the Institute of Charity". He communicated his religious experience and his thoughts to the Countess Maddalena of Canossa.

1826 He left Rovereto for Milan where he resided for two years doing research and writing his work on Politics. He met Count Mellerio [ex-Governor of Milan] and Alessandro Manzoni [the most famous of Italian poets and novelists of the 19th century]. They established very strong friendships for life.

1827 He wrote the first volume of his Theodicy, and other works on Italian Literature.

8th June: he met John Baptist Loewenbruck, a fiery priest from Lorraine, who urged Rosmini to found a new religious Order. They agreed to meet at Calvario of Domodossola, where there was a retreat house and a shrine dedicated to the crucified JESUS.

1828 20th February, Ash Wednesday: Rosmini was alone at Calvario in Domodossola and began a period of prayer and fasting, writing the Constitutions of the Institute of Charity. Loewenbruck joined him much later, in June. The date marked the birth of the Institute of Charity. Rosmini remembered the prophecy made to him years earlier by the Countess

Maddalena of Canossa, "I wish the Sons of Charity to be born between JESUS on the Cross and His sorrowful Mother": the shrine at Calvario had at the back of the main altar the powerful statues of Christ on the Cross and of His sorrowful Mother. November: Rosmini was in Rome, seeking direction from the Pope, and planning to publish in the capital city of Christendom his fundamental works on Spirituality [The Maxims of Christian Perfection] and Philosophy [A New Essay concerning the Origin of Ideas].

1829 15th May: Rosmini's friend, Cardinal Cappellari [later, Pope Gregory XVI], organised the meeting of Rosmini with the Pope, Pius VIII. It was a truly memorable meeting during which the Pope confirmed Rosmini's double mission as a Catholic thinker and as a founder of a new religious Order. The words of the Pope were the following: "It is the will of God that you write books, this is your vocation" and "If you intend to begin in a small way, leaving the Lord to do the rest, we give our approval and are very happy for you to continue".

1830 He published in Rome the Maxims of Christian Perfection and A New Essay concerning the Origin of Ideas. The latter brought him fame and admiration in philosophical circles in Italy and abroad. As Rosmini was recovering in Rome from smallpox, he had a visit from a very talented young solicitor, Luigi Gentili, who wanted to know more about Rosmini and his Institute. After a series of meetings, Gentili took the decision to join the Institute, soon after his ordination to the priesthood in Rome.

31st October: Rosmini, with a small band of brothers and priests, began his novitiate at Calvario following the Rules. He wrote and published Principles of Ethics.

1832-1833 He wrote the book, The Five Wounds of the Church, but he did not publish it. During this time Rosmini laid the foundation for the Sisters of Providence, giving them the Constitutions and receiving their first perpetual vows in the month of October 1838.

1834-1835 Rosmini was parish priest at Rovereto, at the request of clergy and people. He was forced to resign after only one year of intense pastoral work, by the constant harassment of the Austrian police. He wrote the important book on the Renewal of Philosophy.

15th June 1835: Rosmini sent Luigi Gentili with two companions to England at the request of Bishop Baines. It was the beginning of the Institute of Charity in the United Kingdom and Ireland. Rosmini's words to Gentili, "Adopt the English way of life little by little in all that is not sinful".

1837 Rosmini sent the Constitutions of the Institute of Charity to Pope Gregory XVI for formal approval. After months of unexpected difficulties, the Pope gave his full approval on 20th December 1838. In a letter to his brethren, Rosmini said, "How good is the Child JESUS, He has given us today a great gift, adding happiness to happiness". In the Apostolic Letters of Approval, the Pope said of Rosmini: "Antonio Rosmini is a man of eminent intellect, adorned with noble qualities of soul, exceedingly famous for his knowledge of things human and divine, outstanding for his remarkable piety, religion, virtue, probity, prudence and integrity, conspicuous for his wonderful love and loyalty to the Catholic religion and to this Apostolic See".

1839 Rosmini moved his residence to Stresa. He wrote A Treatise on Moral Conscience, which was fiercely opposed by anonymous critics. Rosmini was accused of holding heretical views, and Cardinals and Bishops received copies of slanderous and anonymous booklets written by Eusebio Cristiano (a pseudonym). Rosmini defended his views, but to no avail. It was the start of a long and harsh campaign against Rosmini, with the aim of having Rosmini's works on philosophy and theology condemned by the Church.

1841-1843 Rosmini published The Philosophy of Right, in two volumes, of 1700 pages.

1842 15th January: Rosmini's mother, Giovanna, died at the age of 85.

1843 7th March: Pope Gregory XVI intervened in the ongoing controversy between Rosmini and some members of the Company of JESUS (Jesuits), imposing silence on both parties. The Pope, however, stood by Rosmini, knowing that the attacks against him were caused by jealousy.

1843-1848 A period of relative calm, during which Rosmini dedicated his energy to the Institute of Charity and the Sisters of Providence (Rosminian Sisters). He wrote and published the three volumes of the Theodicy, and other philosophical and theological works.

1847 Rosmini was once again attacked as a heretic of the worst kind, and a collection of 327 propositions taken indiscriminately from his works was published anonymously under the title "Postille". The booklet was sent to Cardinals and Bishops with the request that the works of Rosmini be condemned by the Church.

1848 Rosmini published the Five Wounds of the Church and the Constitutions according to social justice.

3rd August: the Government of Piedmont sent Rosmini to the Pope Pius IX with the double mission of fostering a Concordat between the Church and Piedmont and of persuading the Pope to accept to be the President of a Confederation of free Italian States.

15th August: Pius IX welcomed Rosmini and told him to prepare for the cardinalate. He was told of the intentions of the Pope of appointing him Secretary of State. He had free and frequent access to the Pope.

15th November: the Prime Minister of the Papal States was assassinated signaling the start of an insurrection in Rome. The
Pope was advised to flee the city in disguise and was welcomed in Gaeta by the king of Naples. The Pope gave the order to Rosmini to follow him into exile in Gaeta, with the Pope's brother. Cardinal Antonelli, a staunch supporter of Austria, began his work of discrediting Rosmini in the eyes of the Pope, making life difficult and closing all avenues for Rosmini to even see or talk to the Pope.

1849 January: Rosmini left Gaeta for Naples, to see to the publications of minor works. His enemies took advantage, rushing through the condemnation of two of Rosmini's works: The Five Wounds of Holy Church and The Constitutions according to social justice.

6th of June: The Pope gave his formal approval to the condemnation.

9th of June: Rosmini was back in Gaeta and had an audience with the Pope; Pius IX was kind and friendly, as usual, but did not
mention the condemnation of the two books. Soon after, Rosmini was told by the local police to leave the kingdom of Naples, and he was denied the opportunity of saying goodbye to the Pope.

15th August: Rosmini, on his way back to Stresa, was informed by letter of the condemnation of his two works and
submitted at once in full obedience to the will of the Church.

2nd November: Rosmini was back in Stresa. During the troubled times at Gaeta, Naples, and on the way to Stresa he wrote one of the most profound of his books, The Introduction to the Gospel of St. John.

1850 Rosmini published the Introduction to Philosophy. During the year, a small group of Jesuits re-launched their attack on Rosmini with the anonymous publications of malicious books.

1851 12th March: Pius IX renewed to both opposing parties (Jesuits and supporters of Rosmini) the imposition of silence. The Pope, in his desire to clear the problem once and for all, instructed the Congregation of the Index to examine all the works of Antonio Rosmini.

1854 3rd July: The General Congregation of the Index, presided on the occasion by the Pope himself, declared free from errors all the works of Antonio Rosmini ("Dimittantur Opera Omnia Antonii Rosmini").

1855 22nd February: owing to severe illness, Rosmini was forced to interrupt his work on Theosophy, a profound metaphysical work.

1855 1st July: After a most painful agony which lasted 8 hours, Antonio Rosmini died in the early hours, on the feast of the most Precious Blood of JESUS. He was 58 years old.

1888 Pope Leo XIII condemned 40 Propositions, taken out of context and mainly from the posthumous and unfinished works of Antonio Rosmini, because "they do not seem conformable with Catholic truth".

2001 1st July: The Congregation for the Doctrine of the Faith published a Nota which stated: "'..... It must be recognised that extensive, serious and rigorous scientific literature on Antonio Rosmini's thought has been developed in the Catholic field by theologians and philosophers of various schools of thought, and this has shown that interpretations contrary to faith and Catholic doctrine do not correspond in reality with Rosmini's genuine position.' Further, it concludes that 'the meaning of the [forty] propositions, as understood and condemned by the Decree [Post Obitum] does not in fact pertain to Rosmini's genuine position but to possible conclusions from the reading of his works.'

2006 26th June: The Holy See declared the "heroic virtues" of the Venerable Antonio Rosmini.

2007 18 November: Antonio Rosmini was declared Blessed; he had begun his book on The Five Wounds of the Church on 18th November 1832.

Works of Antonio Rosmini available in English

Introduction to Philosophy
Vol. 1, *About the Author's Studies*

A New Essay concerning the Origin of Ideas, 3 Vol.

Principles of Ethics

Conscience

Anthropology as an aid to Moral Science

Philosophy of Politics, 2 volumes
Vol. 1, *The Summary Cause for the Stability and Downfall of Human Societies*
Vol. 2, *Society and its Purpose*

The Philosophy of Right, 6 volumes
Vol. 1, *The Essence of Right*
Vol. 2, *Rights of the Individual*
Vol. 3, *Universal Social Right*
Vol. 4, *Rights in God's Church*
Vol. 5, *Rights in the Family*
Vol. 6, *Rights in Civil Society*

Psychology, 4 volumes
Vol. 1, *Essence of the Human Soul*
Vol. 2, *Development of the Human Soul*
Vol. 3, *The Laws of Animality*
Vol. 4, *Opinions about the Human Soul*

Theosophy
Vol. 1, *The problem of ontology. Being-as-one*
Vol. 2, *Trine being*
Vol.3, *Trine being* (continued)

Theological language

The Five Wounds of the Church Theodicy

Constitutions of the Institute of Charity Diaries

On Christian Education

The books are available from

ROSMINI PUBLICATIONS
34, Eastdale Road, Carlton, Nottingham,
NG3 7GE

Tel. 0115 841 1420; Mobile 07828781537
pm.dakin@hotmail.com

The Beatification of Blessed Antonio Rosmini Apostolic Letter for the Beatification

"Acceding to the wish of our venerable brother Renato Corti, Bishop of Novara, of many other brothers in the Episcopate and of numerous faithful, and having heard the view of the Congregation of the Causes of the Saints, with our Apostolic Authority we permit that the Venerable Servant of God, Antonio Rosmini, priest, founder of the Institute of Charity and of the Sisters of Providence (Rosminian Sisters), and who, drawing from Divine Wisdom, dedicated himself to the investigation of the mystery of God and of man and moreover spent his whole life in the pastoral ministry, may from now on be called Blessed. His feast may be celebrated in places and in a manner, in accordance with the regulations established by law, on the first of July, the day of his birth to heaven. In the name of the Father, and of the Son, and of the Holy Spirit. Amen

Given at Rome, at St Peter's, on November 15th of the year of the Lord 2007 and the third of my Pontificate."

Pope Benedict XVI

Pope Benedict XVI remembered Blessed Rosmini at the end of the Angelus on Sunday 18th November. This is what he said:

“This afternoon in Novara (Italy), the Venerable Servant of God Antonio Rosmini will be beatified, a great priestly figure and illustrious man of culture, inspired by a fervent love for God and the Church. He witnessed the virtue of charity in all its dimensions and at a high level, but what made him most famous was his generous commitment to what he called “intellectual charity”, which means the reconciliation of reason with faith. May his example help the Church, especially the Italian Ecclesial Communities, to grow in the awareness that the light of human reason and that of Grace, when they journey together, become a source of blessing for the human person and for society.”

Blessed Antonio Rosmini 1797-1855
"There is no true wisdom but in God"

"Rosmini was a great man, too little known today. He was a man of great learning and wisdom... His thinking and spirit ought to be made known and imitated, and perhaps he himself should be invoked as a protector in heaven. We look forward eagerly to the day when that will happen"

(Pope Paul VI).

Autobiography

Antonio Belsito is the Director of Rosmini Publications, a charity trust based in the UK with the objective of making known to the English-speaking world the works of Blessed Antonio Rosmini, who was a great Catholic philosopher, theologian, and spiritual master, as well as being the Founder of the Institute of Charity and of the Sisters of Providence.

After many years of teaching philosophy and theology to students preparing for a University Degree, Antonio Belsito became involved in the direction of Ratcliffe College, whilst at the same time founding and directing the Rosmini Centre House of Prayer in Leicestershire.

As Director of Rosmini Publications, he is dedicated to translating, publishing, and distributing the works of Blessed Rosmini, while, at the same time, lecturing and writing books on the relevance and importance for today of the teaching of Blessed Antonio Rosmini.

A Collective Summary

Antonio Rosmini is the greatest, most original, prophetic Catholic thinker of the last few centuries, little known in the English-speaking world. Following the advice of Popes and Cardinals, he wrote extensively on philosophy, theology, and spirituality, and his teaching is extremely relevant to the major issues confronting the world and the Church of today. His books on spirituality are firmly rooted on Scripture from which they draw the perennial call to holiness, and the means for achieving it through the three steps of purification from sin, constant exercise of the virtues, and union with God. His books on philosophy are full of light for the enquiring mind, ranging from the problem of Truth and Epistemology, to the foundation of Morality, of Right, of Politics, of Natural Anthropology and Natural Religion, and of the Essence of the Human Soul. His work on Theosophy is a most profound study of "being", in its three modes – ideal being, real being, moral being. Faith and Reason, for Rosmini, far from being in opposition are in fact the two wings which allow human beings to rise from the natural to the supernatural world, the one calling on the other, faith calling on reason and reason on faith. His theological masterpiece is undoubtedly the Supernatural Anthropology, which deals with grace, with the "supernatural person", and with the Sacraments. Other important works deal with the Church, in particular with the "wounds" of the Church.

PUBLIC DOMAIN RECORDS AND COPYRIGHT CERTIFICATIONS

THESE ORIGINAL WORKS OF BLESSED ANTONIO ROSMINI HAVE BEEN EDITED BY ANTONIO BELSITO IC. THESE WORKS HAVE BEEN PUBLISHED WITH PERMISSION BY

Rosmini Publications,
200 Leeming Lane North,
Mansfield Woodhouse,
Mansfield, NG19 9EX
United Kingdom

Tel. 0044 (0)1623 402175
0044 7828781537
www.rosminipublications.com
rosminipublications@outlook.com

THE ORIGINAL WORKS OF BLESSED ANTONIO ROSMINI

CREATED BY
CATHOLIC LIFE INTERNATIONAL
BABYLON, NY 11703
www.catholiclifeinternational.org

Printed in the United States of America

CPSIA information can be obtained
at www.ICGtesting.com
Printed in the USA
LVHW081307290520
656931LV00006B/603